DOES ANYONE HEAR OUR CRIES FOR HELP?

Strategies for Successful Living in Difficult Situations

Bertie Ryan Synowiec, M.S.

POSITIVE SUPPORT SEMINARS and PUBLICATIONS
Grosse Ile, Michigan

Other books written by Bertie Synowiec:

Quick and Easy Self-Esteem Builders
Ideario Constructico De La Autoestima
Self-Esteem Builders For Business
Group Facilitation Handbook
Teaching Students Strategies For Survival
    In A Dysfunctional Environment
I'm A Pro At Hard Work
Why Do You Force Me To Talk To A
    Chemical When All I Want Is Your Heart?
Six Tape Series: Helping Kids Succeed in
    School. Guidebook by Bertie Synowiec

Printed on recycled Paper

ISBN 1-885335-03-2

Additional copies may be purchased through

POSITIVE SUPPORT SEMINARS
28641 Elbamar, Grosse Ile, Michigan   48138
313-675-6200   1-800-676-3806

ACKNOWLEDGMENTS

First of all I wish to thank my family and friends, mentors and fellow educators for all the love and support they have given me as I sorted out the lessons I needed to learn on my own personal growth journey.

Having spent most of my life filtering who I was through the eyes of what others thought of me and being controlled by the feelings those incongruities created in me, I now share with you the strategies that have become an integral part of my life as I daily practice believing in myself and detaching in a healthy way from the dysfunctional systems in this world around me.

A very special thank you goes to Dr. Sidney Simon and Suzanne Simon for all their unconditional love and encouragement to take the personal risks that growth requires and for helping me learn to set the boundaries that permitted me to ask for what I needed in my life.

I also wish to thank Steve Dieleman for his support and encouragement to put on paper our shared vision and belief that we can not always pull students or adults in difficult situations from their classrooms, jobs or homes, but must provide these children, their teachers and their parents strategies that will allow them to take care of themselves by separating healthy behaviors from unhealthy ones.

I wish also to thank the unknown authors, whose materials have touched my life in such a way to empower me to share them with you.

And finally my husband and our five children, whose insights and expertise on the family system, have added the finishing touches to this book and who definitely heard and shared my cries for help! As our young daughter once said, "I'm not crying cause I'm hurting; I'm crying because I'm happy we've made us better."

TABLE OF CONTENTS

INTRODUCTION

I am writing this workbook based on insights I have had as an educator for twenty-five years, a parent of five children, grandchild of an alcoholic, the "lost" child in a dysfunctional home due to illness, wife of a spouse with a similar up bringing, and group facilitator and seminar leader in over five hundred communities around the country! These strategies worked for me, as I sought ways to reverse the negative cycles in my life that had robbed me of my self-esteem and caused me to become someone I no longer liked! It has been a ten year journey that started when I began to seriously look at my students at-risk and my children at-risk and my own risky behaviors and see how they were all connected.

It is difficult to love others if we do not first love ourselves. Most adults know they were not taught the skills necessary to identify and cope with the dysfunctional behaviors around them. The question is where to begin? This book will help with that! When I realized that change began with me and saw myself as part of the problem, I knew I was ready to grow and was no longer stuck in my own self-pity.

Since it is not always practical to remove individuals from the difficult situations in which they find themselves, it becomes necessary to teach and to learn the strategies that will allow them to know the difference between what is actually healthy and unhealthy behavior and who owns the problem!

With this information we can then begin to choose what we will, and will not, allow into our lives. Problem ownership, setting boundaries, letting go of the things we cannot control and creating our own reality with healthy detachment is all part of this process that will strengthen our personal power and ability to make positive choices for ourselves.

Bertie Ryan Synowiec
Grosse Ile, Michigan

- CHAPTER 1 -

SETTING THE STAGE FOR RESTRUCTURING AND CHANGE

I began my teaching career fresh, young and full of ideas. As a science teacher, I can clearly remember wanting to clean out the back of the science lab and having the department chairman, who was all of 45 years young, say to me, "Don't bother, it will only get dirty again." I cleaned it anyway.

During the past twenty-five years, I have worn many hats as a teacher and mother of five children. I was always an educator: from full-time public school teacher to replacement substitute teacher, to alternative and adult community educator, special education teacher, group facilitator and professional educational consultant.

Through the years educators were always open to me and shared their true feelings about the changing educational system. Too often they felt that they were being asked to teach and not feel! That was not their job to feel. The incongruities between what they believed and what they were allowed to do brought tremendous stress, anxiety and eventual anger to their jobs.

They began to cry out for help, but everyone became too busy to listen and teachers and teaching became a money issue that could only be resolved with a win-loose competition.

Most of my years in the classroom were spent building self-esteem and helping young people see that they had the potential and ability for success. All my students were "A" students as they entered my classroom, and it was their responsibility to stay at that level. Many did, but there were others who made different choices.

I used study guides to help slower readers and note-taking for the more left brain organized students. I was always aware of the different learning styles of my various students, probably because of my awareness that my own style of learning did not always fit into the traditional educational system. However, as class sizes grew to thirty-five plus, it became more difficult, if not impossible, to individualize their studies.

My classroom was safe, meaning that the students were always free to tell me anything- sometimes too safe for the students, but not always safe for the teacher. My life experiences had taught me to be a listener, very open and willing to learn from them. But, I had missed the lesson on boundaries and consequences for misbehavior.

I also felt that, if they did not succeed, then I must have done something wrong. I always gravitated towards the slower learners and the students who did not fit well into the system. I felt very comfortable with these students.

It was not until I had taught for twenty years and substance abuse was everywhere that the thought entered my mind that the students on chemicals belong in a separate category. With a Masters Degree in Biology and all my teaching credentials and psychology classes, I still knew nothing about these drugs and their effect on the behavior of young people and adults at home, or in the classroom.

I knew plenty of facts connected to the use and abuse of alcohol and other drugs, but I didn't know I knew how it felt to live in such a home. I did not know that any illness, among other situations, could create the same impact on a home. Its effect on behavior, and the consequences of its abuse, were lessons that had not been in my books.

I also remember during my first year of teaching there were a handful of high school students that came in drunk to school, or high on LSD. This was the late 60's. By the early 70's this number increased. I was substituting full time then, and these students would use me as their sounding board.

It seemed *everyone* was using LSD and no one knew, or was even concerned, about the side effects! Some students were very rude and at times out of control, saying awful things about their teachers, or their parents. I did not know it was the drugs speaking. The information was just not available to the general public at that time.

Listening to these seventh and eighth graders, I could not believe the things they told me. It was almost as if, it all was normal for them. I often wonder what we adults were supposed to do with all this information. There seemed to be no rules or regulations. These young people just had a different value system from mine and getting "high" became their goal. Things were just that way.

Our children were small then and the Vietnam War was ending, Martin Luther King and Bobby Kennedy had just been killed and racial tension was high. I was a scared parent and I transferred this to the classroom. I loved teaching and I loved my students, but what was to be their future? I became very protective, never understanding how my need to control was stifling the growth of my students and my children.

It was also difficult to understand why certain teachers from these same dysfunctional classrooms were absent all the time. **Were these the teachers whose co-dependency and constant giving had taken over their lives? Were they exhausted because every day in their classroom they were reliving their childhood?** Were they drowning from their own lack of understanding of the effect of this dysfunctional behavior had on their lives? Were they beginning to feel as if they were the crazy ones?

Today I'm not able to go back fifteen years and ask those questions, but I do know that the issue of job burn out had much to do with the issue of co-dependency which directly affected their self-esteem as educators. We are just now beginning to climb out of the pit we unknowingly dug for ourselves. Pink slips, cut backs, no supplies, and having to work against our own personal value system in order to keep our jobs brought on much anxiety and stress that seemed to accumulate through the years.

Teacher strikes, inflation, and lack of milleage renewals all slowly chipped away and eroded our feelings of self-worth and sense of professionalism. I know this well because I was right in the middle of it. All my degrees and certifications didn't seem to give me the credibility so accepted and expected in the business world. The number of years accumulated teaching meant very little. In fact, at times it was so bad that the attitude was "Oh, you couldn't find a job, so you are teaching."

Being "just a teacher" or "just a parent" was heard everywhere, as the country was preaching zero population growth. It was not enough to be a parent or a mother. It now required more. A second job outside the home was needed to bolster one's self-esteem and help individuals found their identity.

Poor parenting skills and bad teachers were being blamed for all the school drop outs on the streets. No one bothered to look at the addicted youth as children with a disease whose behavior was the fault of the disease. It was not the fault of their parents or their teachers who were absolutely doing the best they could with the tools they had. Drug information was just not available, as it is today. As parents, our children were not born with an owners manual, and as teachers, nothing we ever learned in college could be applied to dealing with these dysfunctional behaviors.

New teaching jobs were totally unavailable so teachers stayed where they were and got quiet, secretly doing their teaching behind closed doors where no one would criticize or judge them. "Good Parents" also stopped talking to their neighbors. So much was happening that they could not understand, and denial was so much safer than facing the reality of the dangers that were really out there for their children. Teachers began to put up their walls, close their classroom doors, guard their secrets and not expose themselves to any criticism, or abuse. Many became isolated and passive.

The students knew their teachers were good and trusted them. They kept their secrets together. They were safe and so was their teacher who perhaps, as a child in school, experienced the same safety away from the dysfunctions of their own family of origin.

They were a team, successful, appreciated, loved, encouraged and never criticized.

At the same time, the adult world outside had changed and become negative. Its positive leaders had become negative powers and those who really wanted to stand up and be counted, began to back down and withdraw to their classrooms and homes. "Let the negativity stay in the teachers lounge, break room, or in the newspapers. I have found myself a safe haven where no one questions my motives and activities." They began to tell themselves, "I will do what I am told and stay where it is safe."

Suddenly more years went by and chemical kids using alcohol and other drugs became more abundant in our classrooms. "Toxic kids" entered the scene from homes where parents were abusing alcohol and other drugs. Many older adults found that they could no longer drink socially, as they had done when they were younger, and they began to moderate their use of alcohol. For some of us, our classrooms, offices, or businesses became un-manageable. Our private lives began to fall apart as our own youngsters entered their teen years and our children at home began to mirror our dysfunctional students in the classroom, or co-workers, and we began to believe that we <u>were</u> the crazy ones.

With this we began to see changes in our personality. The feelings that we had stuffed for years began to leak out in sarcasm and criticism. We seemed to be tired all the time and angry, fearful and less tolerant of those different from ourselves. Who was this monster inside asking all these questions about our right to happiness? Who was this monster inside us that no longer liked kids, administrators, rules, the job, God, or anyone for that matter that brought us to this point in time? "Why do we feel so trapped? Where are we going with our lives? **THERE ARE ONLY EIGHT MORE YEARS UNTIL I RETIRE.**" Now, that's a happy thought!

In a sense we have begun to discover that in giving up all our energy to the concerns of teaching, parenting, peacemaking, directing, doing, owning, controlling, driving, yelling, screaming, crying and getting ill, we were still unable to change the behavior of those around us. Having had little success with these methods, some of our lives continued to be unmanageable. "It has to get better," we would tell ourselves. "I only need to try a little harder!" That didn't work either. Eventually many of us got really tired of always being tired and began to think that it was time to give it all up- all those dedicated, loyal years of working because we felt so powerless over the behavior of others and no matter what we did things did not change!

Does anyone hear our cries for help? Sometimes we wonder. As a teacher and mother of five children, and presently as an educational consultant, I have worked with many communities. I have heard their cries for help as they search for strategies that work with children and adults in difficult situations or environments. It has also been my cry for help as I sought out the answers to questions that related to the incongruities in my life that wore me down.

As you explore the pages of this book, please understand that it is only the beginning of a journey. Whatever excites you, intrigues you, and motivates you, grab hold of it and collect more information. The books contained in the reading list at the back of this book have been very special to me as I discovered new avenues toward a better understanding of the issues in my life that were reflected in the at-risk behaviors in those around me. **ENTER:** The need for educational reform and the restructuring of our lives, schools and businesses.

Education is for children and adults who can hear, feel, trust and talk, but children of Alcoholics and other dysfunctional systems cannot hear, feel trust or talk until the dysfunctional secret is discussed openly, and the guilt, fear and blame is shifted away from the victims!

TRADITIONAL VS. RESTRUCTURED SYSTEMS

The following beliefs compare the Traditional Schools of the past with Restructured Schools of the future. It is provided to us by Bill McKinstry, Superintendent of the Alma School in Michigan.

TRADITIONAL	RESTRUCTURED
Excellence for a few kids	Excellence for all kids
Pessimistic learning	Optimistic learning
Some kids win	All kids win
Remedial programs	Preventive programs
Failure past practice	Success research based
Competitive learning	Cooperative learning
Mystery learning	Mastery learning
Exclusive programs	Inclusive programs
Natural selection process	Talent can be developed
Goals/objectives	Outcomes/proficiency
Stimulus response	Break through thinking
Us vs. them	We
Top down/Hierarchy	Shared consensus
Blame/Critical	Take responsibility
Status quo	Risk takers for change
Academic Focus	Whole child
What is	What ought to be

Page for Notes

"Does Anyone Hear Our Cries For Help?" by Bertie Synowiec

- CHAPTER 2 -

SELF-ESTEEM: WHY BOTHER?

Self-esteem is a by product of the capacity of an individual to deal effectively with one's environment and his/her personal interpretation of the "messages" received from others. It starts to develop early in the life of the child, and extends into pre-school and early elementary grades. Depending on these "messages" and the child's ability to cope with his environment, it can continue to fluctuate throughout his life. Consequently, the teaching of life coping skills through school programs, out of school training and experiential opportunities has become a necessity.

The changing structure of the American family, with the absence of the extended family support system, has increased the need for more personal support within our school systems. In most cases, if the family support system is in place, young people will succeed in spite of the problems existing within a community or school system; but, too often, this support system is not established and the child does not have the "significant other person," or system of support with which to identify.

They feel very alone with a strong need to be accepted and loved. Many of these young people seeking a sense of security turn to substance abuse, violence, pregnancy, and eventual alcoholism to cover up real need for love, support and recognition.

The level of self-esteem and the basic belief of personal worth affects a person's ability to function successfully in a complex world and is the major problem underlying many of the social ills facing our nation. The sense of hopelessness that pervades many of our urban schools and communities causes increased anti-social behavior. Older workers unable to cope with changes in their workplace, younger workers unable to find a productive role and students being unable to see their sense of importance, often can be traced to lack of self-esteem. Anti-social behavior is many times a person's mask. He or she is crying out for help, trying to be recognized and having no sense of direction or goals.

Lack of self-esteem also has a major impact on our economy. As we change our methods to respond to global economic forces, we need a work force that rises to the challenge. Without the confidence that self-esteem brings to a person, the changes and the challenges of tomorrow's workplace will freeze the workers into inaction, rather than inspire them on to new heights.

Crime, drug use, and teen violence often flow from a sense that the person doesn't have a place in the regular world. In school, they would rather be seen as "bad" than "dumb." Without a sense of how to break into the regular adult society and lacking the confidence in themselves to pursue the challenges, young people turn to crime because it gives them a sense of belonging and allows them to achieve a sense of success and achievement.

INDICATORS OF LOW SELF-ESTEEM

Self-Esteem is a belief that you belong, that you will have a rightful place in the society of today and there will be a place for you tomorrow. With this belief that you belong, there is hope. Without it, there is none. People with low self-esteem:

- Have a poor opinion of themselves and often feel put down, or of little worth.

- Feel unlucky, rejected, mistreated and a loser; feel sorry for themselves; have little or no confidence that they can be of value to others.

- Worry something is wrong with them, feel inadequate, think they are good for nothing, are afraid others will find out.

"Does Anyone Hear Our Cries For Help?" by Bertie Synowiec

- Distrusts and feels others are against them and want to hurt them; feel they must defend themselves from others.

- Are uncomfortable when others look or speak to them, can't face up to people confidently, can't look them in the eyes.

- Are insecure with "superior" people, don't feel good enough to be accepted by others, except those who also feel poorly about themselves.

TRAITS OF HIGH SELF-ESTEEM

When the issues around low self-esteem are solved, the following traits of high self-esteem appear and individuals:

- Feel good about themselves and harbor a basic sense of trust in self and others.

- Do not exploit anyone; get along well with other people.

- Can solve their own problems and feel accepted by anybody.

- He a sense of humor and not at the expense of others.

- Form relationships which are mutually enhancing.

- Care about others' welfare, and are able to make positive contributions to others.

- Do not feel sorry for themselves, even though they may have short-comings.

- Celebrate diversity and remain non-judgmental in the presence of those that are different.

ISSUES AFFECTING SELF-ESTEEM

- Needs not met with positive feedback

- Being asked to do more with less

- Media emphasizing the negative

- Financial cutbacks, lack of job security

- No place to be heard or brainstorm feelings

- Lack of recognized achievement resulting in feelings of inadequacy and frustration

- Everyone blaming everyone else as negativity breeds negativity

- Power struggles resulting in lack of spirit, support and teamwork

- Personal issues draining our energy: aging parents, teens, drug abuse

- Working out of one's area of experience

- Diversity misunderstood and judged

- Incongruities in our personal value system

- Stress: No time for care of personal needs

- Lack of respect: unable to please anyone

- People in pain, lashing out at others

- Feelings of isolation and entrapment

- Deadline requirements beyond capability of completion

- Job description that is overwhelming, or no description at all

- CHAPTER 3 -

STRETCHING BEYOND OUR COMFORT ZONE

The issue of change begins with us. My attitude and my thoughts determine how I think, act, or feel. If we are unhappy with how we feel, then it becomes important that we change our thoughts and attitudes toward that which is making us unhappy and recognize that we do have choices. That's the difficult part to accept, yet it all sounds so simple.

The truth is that no matter what our thoughts and attitudes are, they will translate into physical reality. **If we have a good attitude, we will work positively toward a goal and we will get good results. A bad attitude slows us down and we get bad results.**

Educators with their students and business managers with their employees see this all the time. As parents we often live it daily. If we take on the attitude that we cannot do something, then generally, it will not get done until we change our attitude and push ourselves beyond our comfort zone and take the risk to try something new.

A poor attitude can be changed just by taking responsibility for the fact that we have a choice here, and recognizing that we have the power to change our attitude. We can absorb the negativity around us and feel sorry for ourselves or we can detach, consider the source and move on with our lives.

Individuals who believe they are failures are whipped before they even get started. Wouldn't it be great if we could really be convinced that we were all "A" students as they entered a new classroom or a new job? It would then become our choice and responsibility to stay at that level. People with the attitude that they can accomplish whatever they set out to do will work towards the good feeling that success brings when they fulfill their goals.

ACTIVITY #1: <u>Ground Rules for sharing during group discussion</u>: Brainstorm the rules necessary to provide a safe environment where open sharing may take place. These include:

1. All feelings are okay. Feelings are just feelings. They are neither good nor bad.

2. Each person is given time to speak while the rest of the group listens without judgment or criticism.

3. No interruptions or side conversations.

4. When each person is finished others may comment on similar experiences in their lives and the action strategies that have worked for them.

5. Confidentiality must be maintained, except in cases where bodily harm to self or another is discussed (Child Protection Act).

6. Support everyone positively without making fun of anyone.

7. Become one with the group; no one is above anyone else.

8.

9.

10.

11.

12.

ACTIVITY #2: Experiencing your feelings.

* **SIT QUIETLY** and ask yourself the question: "What do I feel inside?

* **THINK ABOUT** what has happened lately to give you this feeling. Ask Yourself: "What caused this feeling?"

* **IDENTIFY** what you need to do. Is this a comfortable feeling? Is it energizing or immobilizing me? Ask yourself: "What should I do about the way I feel?" List all possible choices.

* **LOCATE** the best choice. Ask yourself: "What is the best solution that could be used?"

* **TAKE ACTION** on your best choice.

Remember that we alone can control our feelings. No one makes us feel bad, for example. It is our choice to feel bad - or good. If you do not like your feelings then change your thoughts about that feeling and it will move away.
If you feel that someone "makes you angry" then realize that it is your choice to be angry, or not to be angry, at that person. You will be angry only if you choose to be angry. Let go of it! It will exhaust you and drain you of all your positive energy. Choose instead to think about a favorite hobby, a special friend, or happy experience. You can even think about the weather!

15   "Does Anyone Hear Our Cries For Help?" by Bertie Synowiec

Page for Notes

"Does Anyone Hear Our Cries For Help?" by Bertie Synowiec

- CHAPTER 4 -

TAKING THE RISK TO CHANGE

Risk-taking! It's a new generation! Many of us sit back and watch the risk takers of the world and wonder where they have gotten their energy. Actually the answer is: they have gotten their energy from taking the risk and succeeding.

Think of a time in your life when you took a risk - even to take your first step you risked - and look at the joy walking has brought you through the years. A simple example, yet very clear.

Too many of us have not taken the risk to change anything in our lives for years. Our hair styles, our clothes, our opinion of others outside our circle, our jobs, the way we park our cars, our lesson plans (I had to sneak that last one in!) have not changed for years. We have allowed so much to become predictable, stale and stagnant.

We refuse to learn the computer, the VCR, new math, whole language, cooperative learning. It is too frightening. After all, what if we fail? We cannot risk the chance of being judged by others. It is just not worth it, so we think.

On the other hand, if we choose to slowly become a risk taker, we may be pleasantly surprised at the outcome. We may find we do so well that we may question why it took us so long to let go of our fears and stretch beyond our comfort zone to discover a new exciting world waiting for us. This is where the new energy comes from - the sense of accomplishment and pride we feel when we conquer our fears and become unstuck.

Let's look at some of the issues touching our lives that at times immobilize us and prevent us from making positive choices for ourselves. We all begin with good intentions, but too often find ourselves caught up in negative cycles that we find difficult to break. Understanding how these cycles relate to other hidden issues in our lives that we don't always talk about can be the first step to bringing about positive changes for ourselves and for others. Becoming unstuck, examining how we got there, and rediscovering our energy sources will strengthen our personal power and allow us to move forward with our goals and dreams and focus on our overall wellness.

ACTIVITY #3: Prioritizing feelings. Create a planning board prioritizing the feelings in our lives that seem to be blocking our positive growth. What feelings get in the way and cloud our sense of peacefulness? This activity may be used with your students, employees or children, to help them prioritize the issues controlling their lives.

1. Think for a moment, or brainstorm with your group, the top twelve feelings, or issues, that concern you and write their names in the boxes. The suggestions below may be used.

2. When completed, separate them into twelve pieces of paper.

3. Using the planning board on the next page, place these "feelings" in the boxes, ranking them according to the level at which they take away your energy and distract you from doing the job at hand. For example, if your "anger" is the issue that seems to get in the way the most, place "anger" in the first box marked number one.

4. Share with your partner (or the group) what you found out about yourself that you might want to look at further.

5. As you finish prioritizing the issues, mark a number in the corner of each issue relative to the position you place it for later reference. These positions will change as time goes on and the issues are processed.

PLANNING BOARD: To determine which feelings are acting as road blocks, holding us back from being all that we were meant to be.

1.	7.
2.	8.
3.	9.
4.	10.
5.	11.
6.	12.

ACTIVITY #4: Choosing table topics for group discusion. Look at your planning boards and determine the top six issues that seem to be of greatest interest for the group. These will be used as table topics for discussion. Place one of these in the center of each of the tables. Give individuals an opportunity to get up and walk to the table of their first or second choice. If "anger," for example, requires more space, use it twice and create an additional table for discussion.

- ANGER
- FAULT-FINDING
- CONTROL
- COURAGE
- DETACHMENT
- EXPECTATIONS
- FEEL INADEQUATE
- FRUSTRATION
- GUILT
- HONESTY OF SELF
- LOVE-CONDITIONAL
- PERFECTION
- RESPONSIBLITY
- SELF-DECEPTION
- SELF-RESPECT

- ATTITUDE
- CHANGE
- CONFLICT
- DECISION MAKING
- DESPAIR
- FEAR
- FORGIVENESS
- GIVING TOO MUCH
- GRATITUDE
- LOSS OF CONTROL
- PATIENCE
- RESENTMENT
- SELF-CONTROL
- SELF-ESTEEM
- SERENITY

ACTIVITY #5: Round table discussion. How is the table topic affecting our lives at the present moment?

Procedure: Each individual at the table will be given about two minutes to share their answer to this question while the rest listen without judgment, or criticism. When they are finished others may comment without giving advice, or they may just move on to the next person. When all have shared and this activity has ended, they may return to their original seat.

This exercise may be repeated on a regular basis. The key to selecting the "discussion for that day" will be based on what feelings need to be attended to on that day. As a result, within the group, each time they meet the faces will change at a particular table, but the universality of the feelings discussed will remain the same.

This activity allows participants to see that they are not the only ones having difficulty with a particular issue. The experience of sharing within the group will provide support to one another, as together, we gain the strength to act on our feelings, so that they can no longer keep us "stuck" and inhibit our personal growth.

ACTIVITY #6: Follow-up exercise. Brainstorm the answers to the following:

1. What are some of the problems that arise when we do not deal with our feelings? List.

2. What do you think causes the "acting out" and "bad" behavior? Can we separate the "bad" behavior from the "good" person?

3. How do we avoid confrontation? What type of messages do we use? "You did this. . . " or "I feel that. . ."

4. When these behaviors surface what are some of the successful strategies we have used to take care of ourselves?

As we look at some of these issues, the question arises: Who is really at risk-the child, or the adult? Sometimes those closest to us, or even our children, may "fall between the cracks" and the real issues governing their lives will take over who the person will become, as we blindly question their behaviors.

21   "Does Anyone Hear Our Cries For Help?" by Bertie Synowiec

The following letter exemplifies the question of who is at risk. It was written by a young man, eighteen, who had just graduated from high school. He could not share this story for many years although the experience greatly affected his behavior and attitude toward the educational system.

He became a self-taught learner, separated from his teachers, and had great difficulty fitting into the dysfunctional systems around him that created such pain and misunderstanding.

"Now about my past. It's not as bad as you were led to believe. When I started school I was a very little boy who was very sensitive to himself and the feelings of others. I was everybody's scapegoat. Everyone picked on me to get into fights with and to pick on. I was picked on a lot.

When I got into third grade I reached the absolute bottom of my career. I got a teacher who was the most uncaring person I have ever met in the whole world. She cared about herself and she believed that teaching was just another job. Well, about the third week of school I forgot my homework at home. This was the truth, I really did do it. She didn't believe me and put me out in the hall for the day.

That day, there just happened to be a clown visiting and I had never seen a real clown. visiting the classroom. I never forgave her and never tried to do homework again. At the end of second grade I was one of the top students entering the third grade, I just barely made it into fourth. Fourth grade was a little better..."

What was really going on behind the scenes in this story? Why did it happen? Were they all doing the best they could with the information they had? What was the hidden baggage for the child, his parents or his teacher that day? And who was really at risk? Actually all three were "at-risk."

22   "Does Anyone Hear Our Cries For Help?" by Bertie Synowiec

THE STUDENT: He was a third grader and the oldest of several children. The last baby had just been born into an abusive home, and the expectation for that student was that he be all grown up at age nine. The pressure on him was enormous and he <u>had</u> done his homework. At home there was a lot of activity each morning with a seven, five, three, two year old plus the new baby. The punishment was unjust for the mistake. No one could rescue him.

THE TEACHER: Who knows what caused her/him to over-react and punish that child unreasonably. Was it the frustration of a classroom full of thirty-five forgetful third graders? Was she/he only doing to this young person what had been done to others over the years, or was it learned because the teacher had been punished this way as a young child? Why was the teacher always screaming at the students? Wasn't she or he doing the best they could at the moment even though it was pretty awful?

THE PARENTS: Their co-dependency had affected their relationship and they were fighting to survive and justify their feelings. The husband was gone all the time, leaving the mother alone with all the babies and all the responsibilities without any emotional support.

Was that not how the husband was raised? Wasn't she at risk of drowning in all that she was being asked to be for her family? Who could she talk to for support? There was no time and was she doing as her motherhad done before her?

THE SECRET WAS GUARDED

AND THE DAMAGE WAS DONE.

NO ONE KNEW ANY BETTER.

IT JUST HAPPENED.

"Does Anyone Hear Our Cries For Help?" by Bertie Synowiec

CONFLICT, CONFLICT AND MORE CONFLICT!

CONFLICT OCCURS when we decide to punish others for the pain we feel inside that we are not yet able to express.

CONFLICT OCCURS when we choose not to do our best or not to succeed, to prove to others that we can control our own lives, even though everything seems out of control!

CONFLICT OCCURS when our frustration and anger takes over our lives and causes us to loose control of our actions and the words that come out of our mouth!

CONFLICT OCCURS when nothing else matters but our own survival and we can no longer hear what other are saying due to the pain of our own self-pity and self-centeredness.

WE JUST DIDN'T KNOW

Who is at-risk? How can we know the baggage anyone is carrying when we were taught so well to guard our secrets and not show our feelings?

Didn't we do the best we could with the tools we had? Was it really supposed to be this way?

We just didn't know our choice of profession, as a parent or teacher, would become such a put-down in our lifetime.

We just didn't know our chemically dependent society would produce such unpredictable behaviors

24   "Does Anyone Hear Our Cries For Help?" by Bertie Synowiec

and lead us to believe that we were the crazy ones and that these behaviors may possibly be normal.

We just didn't know that giving up who we were for the approval of others, or our co-dependency as it is called, would drive us to exhaustion and job burnout.

We just didn't know that the role we played in our families when we were growing up would affect the role we took on in our homes and classrooms, as it too became dysfunctional.

We just didn't know that the secrets of our childhood hidden deep in our closets would come out to haunt us in our thirties and forties.

We just did not know anything about dysfunctional systems, chemical abuse, recovery and breaking the cycle.

We just didn't know that substance abuse would become such a problem for so many young people and adults, as to affect their dreams and goals.

We just didn't know the impact "information overload" would have on our well being, and the speed that we would have to go to keep up with a computerized, competitive world.

We just didn't know that our parents would "live to be one hundred" and that we would spend the years after our children were grown, parenting our parents.

We just didn't know that the media would be the "power" that would teach our children a different set of values.

We just didn't know how much all this would affect our self-esteem.

WE JUST DIDN'T KNOW!

Page for Notes

"Does Anyone Hear Our Cries For Help?" by Bertie Synowiec

- CHAPTER 5 -

ISSUES FACING THOSE IN DIFFICULT SITUATIONS

ACTIVITY #7: Prioritizing issues affecting our lives. The format for this exercise is similar to that used with the planning board on the previous pages.Brainstorm as many issues that your group may come up with. Some days this list may be very long and overwhelming. Select the issues that are the most important. Choose the top twelve from your list and work with those on the planning board. When completed, ask the group to list their top six for further group discussion at individual tables. If you are working alone, check the topics that apply to issues affecting your life at this moment.

This exercise permits individuals to look at their issues objectively and begin to live in the present moment, building for their future, and taking each day 'one day at a time,' as they begin to resolve and let go of these issues.

❑ ADDICTIONS	❑ AGING PARENTS
❑ ALCOHOLIC PARENTS	❑ ARGUMENTS
❑ ATTENTION DEFICIT	❑ BOUNDARIES
❑ CHANGED VALUES	❑ DEATH IN FAMILY
❑ DIVORCE	❑ DRUG USE/ABUSE
❑ FORGIVENESS	❑ GRADES
❑ ISSUES OF CONTROL	❑ ILLNESS
❑ JOB - MONEY	❑ LEARNING
❑ LONELINESS	❑ NEGATIVITY
❑ PARTIES	❑ PEER PRESSURE
❑ PHYSICAL ABUSE	❑ POLITICS
❑ RELATIONSHIPS	❑ RELIGION
❑ ROOMMATES	❑ SELF-ESTEEM
❑ SEXUALITY	❑ SEXUAL ABUSE
❑ SOCIAL ISSUES	❑ STEP PARENTS
❑ TEEN SUICIDE	❑ TIME

PLANNING BOARD: Prioritize the major issues affecting our lives.

1.	7.
2.	8.
3.	9.
4.	10.
5.	11.
6.	12.

MY MASK
by Kevin P. Synowiec

I wish you could see me.
You say hello here and there,
But you don't see who I really am.

It's not your fault, though.
I put up a defense
To protect myself from harsh words,
To shield me from blinding phrases.
When I witness them, my shield goes up.
I act like someone else.
I've become a master of imitation.

I feel like a fake.
Do you see this smile?
This is my number one disguise.
I have many more.
You see, inside of me,
There is loneliness and pain,
A pain no one knows about.
Possibly the suffering of a lost child.

Maybe, I am who you see.
That's my best trick...
That's how you're supposed to see me.

Maybe, it is my fault.
Am I just shy? Why?
What's wrong with me?
I feel unfinished,
Broken. Removed.

Are we all in this together?
Do you wear a mask too?
I think someday I will take mine off
Just to see what it's like.
Why am I so nervous though?
I want to take off my mask completely,
But I don't know how.

ACTIVITY #8: Risk-taking group exercise. Take a few minutes to write about the following and share your answers with a partner, as time permits.

1. Write down something about a turning point in your life.

2. Describe a person that has had a tremendous impact upon your life.

3. Do you give more of your time and energy to others than you take back for yourself? Do you like to save people?

4. Are you more of a care-giver than a receiver and are you able to take a compliment?

5. What issue in your life is of great importance to you, something you feel very strongly about?

6. Think for a moment about another person that you have empowered. Describe what you did to motivate them to look at themselves and change their behaviors.

ACTIVITY #9: <u>Writing a letter of gratitude</u>: Write a letter of gratitude **to yourself** from that special person that you empowered, or helped become a better person. Most often, these thank you letters are never written by that person, even though you know they were grateful for all that you did for them. Describe what you did for them and share your success, as it helped them to focus and have a sense of purpose.

Format: Write as quickly as you can, without thinking of your spelling, or punctuation. This is a letter to you from that special person that you empowered to find their place in this world.

Dear _____,

I know that you have done so much for me and that I have never taken the time to thank you. I want to do that now. . . .

CO-DEPENDENCY: WHAT IS IT?

Co-dependency is destructive to our health and well-being when we give up who we are for the approval of someone else. John Bradshaw and Melody Beattie, among others, have written many wonderful books on this subject which has much to do with making positive choices for ourselves.

As we read the following, we will see that many care-givers have been trained to behave as co-dependents. "Love your neighbor as yourself," a well established rule, really says that you cannot love your neighbor until you love yourself. You cannot give what you do not have.

I am co-dependent when:

- My good feelings about who I am stem from being liked by you and by receiving your approval.

- Your struggles affect my serenity or peacefulness. My mental attention focuses on solving your problems or relieving your pain.

- My mental attention is focused on trying to please you and protect you and I try to manipulate you to help me.

- My own hobbies and interests are put aside. My time is spent sharing your interests and hobbies.

- How I feel about myself depends on how good you look. I only feel good when you feel good, as I feel you are a reflection of me.

- I am not aware of how I feel; I am aware of how you feel.

- I am not aware of how I feel or what I want. I am aware of how you feel and ask you what you want. If I am not aware, I assume.

- The dreams I have for my future are linked to you.

- My fear of rejection determines what I say or do. My fear of your anger determines what I say or do.

- I use giving as a way of feeling safe in our relationship.

- My social circle diminishes as I involve myself with you.

- I put my values aside in order to connect with you. I value your opinion and way of doing things more than my own.

- The quality of my life is in relation to the quality of yours.

Author unknown

WHO YOU ARE DOES NOT DEPEND

ON WHAT OTHERS THINK OF YOU!

A HEALTHY SELF-IMAGE:
WHAT CREATES IT?

ACTIVITY #10: Creating a healthy self-image.
Create a list of healthy behaviors from the co-dependency list of behaviors on the previous page.

    We become healthy when we make choices to believe in who we are, as important individuals, and begin again to take care of ourselves, regardless of what others may say, or think.
    We need to trust our own value system and follow its lead to take charge of our lives, as we had before we let others control us and destroy our feelings of self-worth.

• _____

• _____

• _____

• _____

• _____

• _____

• _____

• _____

• _____

• _____

• _____

• _____

• _____

- CHAPTER 6 -

OUR SELF-ESTEEM

ACTIVIY #11: **Our self-esteem.** Taking a look at who we are and separating it from what we do, often requires risk-taking and true honesty with ourselves. This exercise is for you alone in a quiet place where you can look at who you are and how you feel about yourself.

- Who am I? What kind of person am I?

- Do I like and enjoy being myself, or would I rather be someone else?

- What am I good at doing? What do I know that I really do well?

- Do I believe that I am important enough to take time for myself? What do I enjoy doing?

- How do I feel when I receive a compliment? Do I brush it off or accept it openly?

- Do I need people around me all the time or can I be at peace when I am by myself?

- Do I make impossible demands on myself?
  Is excellence okay or does everything have
  to be perfect?

- What are my goals in life? Are they realistic?

Remember that we are able to create our own reality with positive choices. Low self-esteem is acquired. It can be changed. We place so many conditions on our self-love: "If I were thinner. . .If I didn't have those freckles. . . If my hair were straight, I would like me more."

If we wish others around us to be healthy and have good self-esteem then we must model that same good self-esteem for them. We cannot be complaining and fault-finding all the time and expect them not to do the same. "Don't do as I do, but do as I say." does not work today.

You will be caught in the discrepancies of your behavior and be seen as weak, or as a liar, because others will discuss and analyze your actions. "It is not fair," they will say. "If you cannot take responsibility for your actions, why should I?" It almost seems necessary in this changing world, where the only thing constant is change, to look first at ourselves!

For this reason it becomes important that we first take care of ourselves, so that we will have the energy to choose to give to others. Take a look at the advertisement on the next page. We sure have come a long way since that one was placed!

> **WHO WE ARE IS MORE THAN OUR GRADES IN SCHOOL. WHO WE ARE IS MORE THAN WHAT WE DO.**

WANTED
•••••

GOOD WOMAN

MUST BE ABLE TO
CLEAN, COOK, SEW,
DIG WORMS AND
CLEAN FISH.

MUST HAVE BOAT
AND MOTOR.

PLEASE SEND
PICTURE OF BOAT
AND MOTOR.

UNCONDITIONAL ACCEPTANCE OF SELF

ACTIVITY #12 : Your letter of recommendation written by you. Although it may seem uncomfortable at first, do not be humble. List all your great qualities.You are the only one who really knows how you have touched the lives of others. Now is your chance! Let the words flow out of your head onto your paper, writing all those wonderful things you alone know you have done.

Dear _____,

I feel so honored to have the opportunity to tell you about_____. _____ has truly touched my life. Let me tell you more. . .

IN WHICH HOUSE DO YOU LIVE?

"I got two A's," the small boy cried,
His voice was filled with glee.
His father bluntly asked,
"Why didn't you get three?"

"Mom, I've got the dishes done!"
The girl called from the door.
Her Mother very calmly said,
"Did you sweep the floor?"

"I've mowed the grass," the tall boy said,
"And put the mower away!"
His father asked him, with a shrug.
"Did you clean off the clay?"

The children in the house next door
Seem happy and content.
The same things happened over there,
But this is how it went:

"I got two A's," the small boy cried,
His voice was filled with glee.
His father proudly said, "That's great!
I'm glad you live with me!"

"Mom, I've got the dishes done!"
The girl called from the door.
Her mother smiled and softly said,
"Each day I love you more."

"I've mowed the grass," the tall boy said,
"And put the mower away!"
His father answered with much joy,
You've made my happy day!

Children deserve a little praise
For tasks they're asked to do.
If they're to lead a happy life.
So much depends on you.

Anonymous

"Does Anyone Hear Our Cries For Help?" by Bertie Synowiec

Page for Notes

- CHAPTER 7 -

THE FAMILY SYSTEM

As family members struggle to guard their family secrets within a home, their family system can become dysfunctional until the "secret" is revealed and the problem acknowledged.

WHAT CAN CAUSE A FAMILY TO BECOME DYSFUNCTIONAL?

- Physical abuse
- Sexual abuse
- Illness
- Alcoholism
- Workaholic
- Too many rules
- Fighting/Violence
- Relocation, etc.

- Unemployment
- Co-dependency
- Death in family
- Chemical Abuse
- Not enough rules
- Divorce, Separation
- Teenage parents

ROLES WITHIN THE FAMILY SYSTEM

Dysfunctionalism may cause young people and adults to take on certain roles within a family, as they struggle to guard these secrets and maintain a balanced family system that looks good on the outside. **Although these family positions are present in healthy families, these roles become accentuated in a dysfunctional home**.

Family members seem to be thrown into a particular position without a choice, and remain trapped in that role until the secret is revealed, and the blame shifted away from the individuals and placed on the actual cause of the problem.

These accentuated positions of family members in a chemically dependent family have been well documented through the work of Claudia Black, Sharon Wegscheider-Cruse, Virginia Satir, Melody Beattie and others.

1. THE SCAPEGOAT is often the target of family frustrations and confusion and the main focus is on his/her misbehavior, rather then the secret.

Behavior	Feelings
Gets blamed for everything	Angry and hurt
Appears hostile, defiant	Alone, frightened
Withdrawn, artistic	Rejected, trapped
Seeks negative attention not trustworthy	Medicates pain with drugs
Irresponsible, unpredictable	Misunderstood

2. THE FAMILY HERO/RESPONSIBLE CHILD is the child whose mission in life is to make the family look good and compensate for the families imperfections! Often they are all grown up at age five.

Behavior	Feelings
Takes over parent roll, protects family secret	Inconsistency- an adult-child
Takes charge of situations, high achiever in school encouraged by adults	Feels "above" his/ her immature peer group
Always does it right	Isolation, rejection lonely, angry
Puts others first at own expense	Externally he/she is fine, fine, fine
Blames the scapegoat for mess they're in	Internally feels constant need for perfection

OUR FAMILY HERO
The University Wouldn't Take Him

He's been an adult since he was four. He took care of his Mom and Dad, sisters and brothers; it consumed a lot of his time and made him responsible, *but the University wouldn't take him.*

He's such a caring person, always giving, reaching out, trying to help others. He wants to go into counseling, industrial psychology, working with white collar workers and helping families to get along better—he's been in training some seventeen years now, *but the University wouldn't take him.*

His GPA is only a 2.5, at least that's what he thought, until they knocked off all his "right-brain" classes that weren't college-prep enough. Three intense years of Mechanical Drawing and Architectural Design; four years of Band, eight hours a week; Regional Honors Choir, Madrigals, Musical Productions, along with hours of memorizing music and lines. *Guess he didn't learn anything worthwhile there!*

Three years of Math and two years of Science—Physics can wait until college. He's been sailboat racing with aerodynamic agility since he was seven and sailed in the three hundred and fifty mile Lake Huron to Mackinaw Race these past four years, *but the University thought he lacked the discipline to study—after all his grade point wasn't high enough.*

Boy, can he write about his feelings straight from his heart and share for hours on end, but his Freshman English Communications class didn't count either, and Basic Accounting, what good was that? *So the University threw them all out and said, "Not enough academics to enter our doors!"*

Life Skills! Life Skills! They just don't count for college entrance! Driven to fix his car, he read the manuals and rebuilt the engine (not to mention the carburetor, master cylinder, brakes and power steering pump.) I often wonder, if a four point student can do that, too. *The University didn't want him. With grades like his, they said he can't possibility meet the challenges of a stressful year.*

Oh, and his personal commitment: his feelings about substance abuse, suicide, violence, God, religion, and life! What do they know about what he knows? There is no measurement, no grade for integrity or determination. *The University wouldn't take him; his grade point wasn't high enough.*

An out-of-state private college grabbed him and gave him an eight thousand dollar competitive music scholarship for four years. *They looked at the whole person and all of his talents and capabilities, not just his English, Math, Science and History grades because they knew what they were getting— afterall, they had educated his parents!*

3. THE MASCOT, OR CLASS CLOWN takes on the burden of cracking a joke when the family situation gets tense. This child may be learning disabled with a lot of energy that is often misunderstood.

Behavior	Feelings
Charming, yet fragile	Fears being found out and maybe
Family clown, hyperactive	not being funny enough to save
Does anything for attention	the situation
Super cute, humorous,	Fears that he is the crazy one
Overly dependent	Immature, lonely confused

ANTS IN MY PANTS

"They told us today in school that if we can't sit still we won't get to go with our class to Washington D.C. this year. They told us that our teachers will get together and decide who can go and who can't. It's only the second week in school and I already know I won't go. They'll all talk about me and decide since I can't sit still, that I can't go...

"Mommy, why is it that they don't understand that I can't sit still. Don't they know that my moving helps me concentrate and focus - that silence allows my mind to wander, and noise helps me find the words on the page?"

Why am I so different? My friends who play sports with me are different too. Most of us have taken Ritalin. I did too, until my teacher asked if I took my pill yet? There's no way I'm going to take drugs! I'll make it without them... I can do it! If I just work harder and longer I'll get my work done.

"Settle down!" "Sit down!" "Pay attention!" "Stop rocking!" "Stop fidgeting!" "Stop moving!" "Stay in your seat!"- I wonder if all adults could sit in these hard, uncomfortable chairs all day from 8:15 until 3:15 with only seven five minute breaks and thirty-five minutes for lunch?

"Mom, you've always allowed me to use my energy to do things... to run, to build tree forts, to bike, to sail, to play basketball... You taught me to learn with my hands and my eyes and ears." Following the line on the page is so difficult for me. Each word creates a new vision, a new and different thought, a new story, a new dream to take me away...

I read the sports section daily in the newspaper; I love the video of "Roots;" Shop was seriously fun; Band and Drumming is great! Heck, it beats sitting still... Oh, how my body aches; I feel so defeated... My

45   "Does Anyone Hear Our Cries For Help?" by Bertie Synowiec

energy is being wasted in me... I want my dreams and my creativity to fly.

When is enough enough? And then to have to sit still on the bus? I come home exhausted from fighting my inner drive for movement and expression. I collapse into the couch, completely drained, and begin my homework. . .   ©1989 Bertie Synowiec

4. THE LOST OR QUIET CHILD creates a fantasy world as she/he wishes it to be and silently escapes from the realities of the dysfunctional world in which she/he lives, pretending that everything is fine, fine, fine.

Behavior	Feelings
Quiet, good, hides	Appears happy
Retreats into a fantasy world	Fears being left alone, helpless
Does not get involved	Abandonment
Does nothing, says nothing	Has difficulty with primary
Avoids trouble, withdrawn	relationships and is not sure
Works well alone	where they fit into the family

The "family system" in a chemically dependent home, school and workplace creates co-dependent relationships that perpetuate the dysfunction by enabling the "bad" behavior to continue. As we observe these individuals, we need to help them become comfortable with the issue of sharing, as we become comfortable ourselves. Being vulnerable always meant being weak to most of us; yet, it is the asking for what we need that brings others closer to us, thus, making us stronger.

feelings. Their loyalty to the family bond, or their situation, is strong, and they will guard their secrets, until they no longer have the energy to stay on the roller coaster because of the pain. Then, as friends and peer listeners, we have the opportunity to reach out and support them, as they begin their journey toward recovery.

> **DENIAL IS PART OF THE DISEASE OF ALCOHOLISM AND SLIPPING BACK INTO OLD PATTERNS, IS PART OF THE RECOVERY PROCESS.**

Denial is part of the disease caused by chemical dependency and it does not just belong to one member of the family. We need to accept this and to stop blaming ourselves for not being able to convince others with all the facts. They cannot hear the facts. They are too scared and defensive and insecure to listen. If they accept this information then what will happen to them and their family? Who will love them and take care of them? It is much easier to deny the problem, then it is to act on it. "It's not that bad. I can cope. I have coped this long. My father/mother was the same way. I can handle it."

What most people fail to realize is that once they get past their denial, they can really get the help and support they need to bring about change for themselves. They are able to create their own reality with positive support from people who will share their vision to continue to grow.

> **WE CANNOT CHANGE ANOTHER PERSON. WE CAN ONLY CHANGE OURSELVES. THAT CHOICE TO CHANGE OR TO NOT CHANGE IS THEIR'S ALONE.**

FORMS OF DENIAL

MINIMIZING - Admitting to some degree that there is a problem, but in such a way, that it appears to be much less serious than it actually is.

RATIONALIZING - Offering alibies, excuses, justifications, etc. The behavior is not denied, but an inaccurate explanation of its causes are given.

PROJECTION OR BLAMING - Denying responsibility for certain behaviors or feelings, maintaining that the responsibility lies with someone, or something else (people, places and things.) other than themselves.

INTELLECTUALIZING - Avoiding emotional, personal awareness of the problem or chemical dependency by dealing with it on a level of generalization, intellectual analysis or theorizing.

DIVERSION - Changing the subject to avoid a topic that is threatening.

HOSTILITY - Becoming angry and irritable when reference is made to personal chemical usage and its relating behavior.

WITHDRAWAL - Resorting to silence, or a depressive state, whenever discussion of the drinking problem is experienced.

COMPLIANCE - Offhandedly complying to the acceptance of what's being stated. The "YES" man or woman. Should not be confused with "acceptance and surrender."

FATALISTIC - Admitting alcohol, or other drugs is a problem, but refusing to do anything about it:" So what? I'll drink myself to death."

RIGID - Alcohol/drugs is not the problem: "I don't want to hear about my drinking." "It's all your fault, anyhow."

ALTERNATE FOCUS - Alcohol is part of it, but the real problem is _____.

Author Unknown

WHAT QUALIFIES THE PROBLEM DRINKER?

To determine whether a person is a problem drinker, ask him, or her, to answer, as honestly as possible, the following questions. This can also be used with young people to heighten their awareness to the dangers of use and abuse of alcohol and other drugs. These test questions have been used by John Hopkins University Hospital, Baltimore, Maryland, to determine whether a patient is a problem drinker.

Yes/No   Question

__ __ Do you lose time from work due to drinking?
__ __ Is drinking making your home life unhappy?
__ __ Do you drink because you are shy with other people?
__ __ Is drinking affecting your reputation?
__ __ Have you ever felt remorse after drinking?
__ __ Have you gotten into financial difficulties as a result of drinking?
__ __ Do you turn to lower companions and an inferior environment when drinking?
__ __ Does your drinking make you careless of your families welfare?
__ __ Has your ambition decreased since drinking?
__ __ Do you crave a drink at a definite time daily?
__ __ Do you want a drink the next morning?
__ __ Does drinking cause you difficulty sleeping?
__ __ Has your efficiency decreased since you've been drinking?
__ __ Is drinking jeopardizing your business/job?
__ __ Do you drink to escape worries and trouble?
__ __ Do you drink alone?
__ __ Have you ever had a complete loss of memory as a result of drinking?
__ __ Has a physician treated you for drinking?
__ __ Do you drink to build up your self-esteem?
__ __ Have you ever been in a hospital or institution on account of drinking?

If you have answered **YES** to any *one* of the above questions, there is a definite warning that you may have a drinking problem. If you have answered **YES** to any *two* of the questions, the odds are that you are a problem drinker. If you have answered **YES** to *three or more* of the questions, you definitely are a problem drinker....

WILL SHE (HE) EVER STOP YELLING?

I think she (he) did for a while--
    or was I too busy to notice it was still there?

It's been months now--
    I know she (he) wants to leave, but what would
    the neighbors or her (his) family think?

She's (he's) so unhappy--
    and has no idea that he's responsible for
    her (his) own happiness.

She (he) thinks that's my job--
    along with many others I've failed at in her (his)
    eyes.

That's why she (he) yells--
    Nothing is right in her (his) life: Kids do not show
    their respect to her (him) either.

That's my fault too--
    I taught them that, she (he) believes.
    What power she (he) gives me!

Now I just back away--
    Unfortunately the bomb still goes off.
    She (he) finds me.

I would never create the mess she (he) says we live in--
    the pain, the deliberate hurts and cruelty.

Why would I?--I'm a pacifist and have worked so
    heard to find my own inner peace.

- CHAPTER 8 -

CHEMICAL KIDS/TOXIC KIDS

"**Chemical kids**" are young people, or adults, whose personal growth stopped with the first drink and who are currently using and abusing chemical substances, prescription drugs, or alcohol. Any one of the following signs is cause for concern. As our awareness to this issue is heightened, we see them everywhere. Some adults were married and divorced three years before they realized that their breakup was caused by the craziness of alcoholism.

If several signs are noted, or if only one sign is frequently seen by a friend or family member, it is recommended that the person contact Al-anon for more information so that they may become involved with a support group that understands, uncon-ditionally, the difficulties they are having and will help them to find the answers and strength to take care of themselves so that they may take care of their child, student, friend, or family member. Twelve step programs work and have been in existence since the mid-nineteen twenties. The faces of the individuals in the group have changed, but the feelings, stories, and issues have not.

Since it is not always practical to remove young people from the dysfunctional system in which they find themselves, we in a restructured school system must now teach them the coping skills that will allow them to set boundaries and recognize ownership of the problem. There are definitely strategies to be learned. We adults might as well learn them in the process. This is not always easy because, at first glance, the skills seem contrary to the belief system that emphasized the control we spent years to develop.

Young people and adults need to separate the bad behavior caused by the drug from the good person who has been changed by this disease.

People working, or living with chemical youth or adults, need to shift ownership of the problem to the alcohol or other chemicals. **ALCOHOLISM IS A DISEASE AND IT IS THE DISEASE THAT IS TALKING.** Individuals living with or working with difficult people need to focus on not reacting to the behavior, or owning the problem. They did not cause the behavior. The drug did that for them. It is the disease talking and although they can not always get away from the put downs and negativity, they can make positive choices for themselves regarding where they will spend their energy and what they will internalize.

This takes practice and it is an achievable goal as co-workers, family members, teachers and friends, heighten their awareness to the need to change the enabling behavior that allows the bad behavior to continue.

Young people become the **"toxic children"** in our schools and homes as they slowly are poisoned by the indirect affects of this disease on them, as they try to sort out the unpredictable behaviors around them. Without the substance they may begin to imitate the "poison behavior." Because of the incongruities that they just cannot understand, they may begin to act out and use various coping strategies in order to survive. As they get older they may choose to medicate their pain by using and abusing substance.

Chemical kids are people whose use of alcohol and other drugs has begun to take over their lives. All high school teachers have had these students in their classrooms. Many parents and educators look at the following behaviors as normal for adolescents and have difficulty believing that it could be their child

Chemical abusers are absolute masters of deception. As time goes on because denial is so much easier, those with the problem are the last to know they have a problem. Intervention, which brings family members, or significant individuals together to confront the issue, may be necessary.

SIGNS OF A PROBLEM - Chemical kids

- **A DROP IN GRADES** - Slow or sudden, poor performance, skipping, sleeping in class.
- **SWITCHING FRIENDS** - Seeing a different group of friends, or ones you may object to, or not bringing their new friends around at all.
- **EMOTIONAL HIGHS AND LOWS** - Easily upset, rapid, unpredictable, emotional changes, doesn't seem as happy as they used to be.
- **DEFIANCE OF RULES** - Pushing limits, many excuses for staying out late, not coming home.
- **BECOMING MORE SECRETIVE** - Not sharing or only sharing a few personal problems.
- **LOSS OF INITIATIVE/WEIGHT CHANGES** - Less energy, sleeping more, drastic weight loss
- **WITHDRAWING FROM FAMILY FUNCTIONS**- Camping, church, meals, family gatherings.
- **CHANGE IN PHYSICAL HYGIENE** - Sloppy, wearing the same clothes for days.
- **NOT INFORMING YOU OF ACTIVITIES** - Open houses, teacher meetings, suspensions.
- **ISOLATION** - Possibly spending a lot of time in his/her room.
- **SUSPICION OF MONEY OR ALCOHOL MISSING** - From parents, brothers, sisters.
- **SELLING POSSESSIONS** to gain money - Clothing, records, gifts; has money, but no job.
- **FEELING MANIPULATED AND BARGAINED WITH** - Playing one parent against the other.
- **SHORT TEMPERED AND DEFENSIVE** - When confronted about behavior, or other concerns. Becomes angry often, has a short fuse.
- **LEGAL PROBLEMS** - Driving while intoxicated, curfew violations, attends parties broken up by police.
- **FINDING PARAPHERNALIA** - Papers, pipes, clips, drugs, bottles.
- **ABUSIVE BEHAVIOR** - Verbally or physically.
- **COMING HOME FROM SCHOOL/WORK, DRUNK/HIGH** - Always cause for concern, slurred speech, unusual giddiness, smelling of pot/ alcohol.

"Does Anyone Hear Our Cries For Help?" by Bertie Synowiec

COMMON PERSONALITY CHANGES

The following personality changes can occur due to drug/alcohol abuse, or other inherited dysfunctional behaviors learned from previous generations. The expression "I want my son, daughter/spouse/parent back again" is indicitive of the following personality changes that bury the true personality of the chemically dependent individual.

- Self-centered - King of the mountain
- Sudden unpredictable sharpness
- Acute negativity and frustration with others
- Outbursts of violent, dangerous behavior
- Sexual abuse, incest, date rape
- Lack of respect for someone else's boundaries
- Personality switches from being apologetic, gentle, loving to that of being angry, angry, angry
- Verbally abusive, puts everyone down
- Insecure, defensive, low self-esteem
- Irresponsible, broken promises
- Denial of their reality, lies
- Aggressive, controlling, righteous
- Blaming everyone else for his/her mistakes
- Exhausted, drained of energy, hurting inside
- Functional— goes to work/school and is dysfunctional later
- Dysfunctional - looses job, drops out of school, family, society
- Looks to the dark side of life, is very negative
- Inappropriate language
- Is unaware that their behavior hurts others
- Their life is unmanageable and they are usually the last to know
- Controlled by a compulsion, or addiction that changes who they really are
- Denies use and abuse of drugs

AS A YOUNG PERSON
DO YOU NEED ALATEEN?

Yes/No *Please mark yes, or no, as the answer applies to you.*

❑ ❑ Do you have a parent, friend or relative with a drinking problem?

❑ ❑ Do you feel you got a rotten break in life?

❑ ❑ Do you hate one or both of your parents?

❑ ❑ Have you lost respect for your non-alcoholic parent?

❑ ❑ Do you try to get even with your parents when you think they have been unfair?

❑ ❑ Are you ashamed of your home?

❑ ❑ Do you wish your home could be more like the homes of your friends?

❑ ❑ Do you lose your temper a lot?

❑ ❑ Do you sometimes say and do things you don't want to but can't help yourself?

❑ ❑ Do you have trouble concentrating on school work?

❑ ❑ Do yor resent having to do jobs around the house that your parents should be doing?

❑ ❑ Are you afraid to let people know what you're really like?

❑ ❑ Do you sometimes wish you were dead?

❑ ❑ Are you starting to think it would be nice to forget your problems by taking drugs or getting drunk?

❑ ❑ Is it hard for you to talk to your parents? Do you talk to them at all?

❑ ❑ Do you go to extremes to get people to like you?

❑ ❑ Are you afraid of the future?

❑ ❑ Do you believe no one could possibly understand how you feel?

❑ ❑ Do you feel you make your alcoholic parent drink?

❑ ❑ Do you stay out of the house often because you hate it there?

❑ ❑ Do you get upset when your parents fight?
❑ ❑ Do you avoid telling your parents the truth?
❑ ❑ Do you worry about your parents?
❑ ❑ Are you nervous or scared alot of the time?
❑ ❑ Do you resent the alcoholic's drinking?
❑ ❑ Do you feel nobody really loves you or cares what happens to you?
❑ ❑ Do you feel like a burden to your parents?
❑ ❑ Do you sometimes do strange, shocking things to get attention?
❑ ❑ Do you cover up your real feelings by pretending you don't care?
❑ ❑ Do you take advantage of your parents when you know you can get away with it?

If you are a teenager and answered "yes" to some of the above questions or if you are close to someone with a drinking or other drug problem, Alateen may help you.

Adapted from: **ALATEEN - HOPE FOR CHILDREN OF ALCOHOLICS**, 1973. Compiled and distributed by: Al-Anon Family Group Headquarters, Inc. P.O. Box 182, Madison Square Station, N.Y., N.Y. 10159.

TYPES OF BEHAVIOR
Chemical kids/Toxic kids

LOW SELF-IMAGE — has poor opinion of self, often feels put down or of little worth, a loser, rejected, mistreated; feels sorry for self; has no confidence that he or she can be of value to others. • Worries that some-thing is wrong with him/her, feels inadequate, thinks he/she is good for nothing, is afraid others will find out "how bad I really am." • Distrusts others, feels they are against him/her and want to hurt him/her, feels they must defend self from others. • Is uncomfortable when people look at or speak to them. Can't look at people confidently and look them in the eyes. Is insecure with "superior" people, doesn't feel good enough to be accepted by others, except those who also feel poorly about themselves.

INCONSIDERATE OF OTHERS — does things that are damaging to others. • Does things that hurt people, enjoys putting people down. • Acts selfishly, doesn't care about the needs or feelings of others. • Seeks to build up self by manipulating others for his own purposes. • Takes advantage of weaker persons and those with problems. • Won't help other people, except, possibly, family members or close friends.

INCONSIDERATE OF SELF — does things that are damaging to self. • Puts self down, brings anger and ridicule on self. • Acts as though they don't want to improve self, or solve problems. • Tries to explain away problems, or blames them on somebody else. • Denies, hides from and runs away from problems. • Doesn't want others to point out problems or talk about them, resists help.

AUTHORITY PROBLEM — does not want to be managed by anyone. • Views authority as an enemy camp "out to get him/her." • Resents anyone telling them what to do, does not accept advice from anyone. • Can't get along with authority figures, confronts them often over minor matters. • Does not respond well to parental control or supervision. • Tries to out-maneuver authority figures, circumventing or manipulating them.

MISLEADS OTHERS — draws others into negative behavior. • Seeks status by being a negative or delinquent leader. • Gives support to the negative or delinquent actions of others. • Misuses others to achieve own goals, getting them to do his/her "dirty work." • Wants others to be in trouble with him/her, afraid of being separate. • If others follow and get in trouble, feels it is their problem and not his or hers.

EASILY MISLED — drawn into negative behavior by others. • Can't make own decisions and is easily controlled by stronger persons. • Can't stand up for what they believe, even when they know they are right. • Is easily talked into committing delinquent acts in order to impress others. • Behavior varies from good to bad, according to influence from associates. • Lets people misuse them, is willing to be somebody else's flunky.

AGGRAVATES OTHERS — treats people in negative, hostile ways. • Makes fun of others, tries to embarrass them and make them feel low. • Seeks attention in negative ways, irritates or annoys people. • Makes subtle threats in word or manner. Challenges others • Hassles, intimidates, bullies and pushes people around.

EASILY ANGERED — is often irritated, or provoked, or has tantrums. • Frequently becomes upset or explosive but may try to excuse such behavior as naturally "having a bad temper." • Easily frustrated, unable to accept failure or disappointments. • Responds to slightest challenge or provocation, thus owning others' problems • So sensitive that he can't stand criticism or one disagreeing with him/her. • Easily upset if someone shouts at him/her, or points a finger, touches, or shows any negative feelings toward him/her.

STEALING — takes things that belong to others. • Thinks it is all right to steal if you are sneaky enough not to get caught. • Doesn't respect others and is willing to hurt another person to get his/her own way. • Steals to prove he or she is big and important, or to prove he is "slick" enough to get away with it. • Steals because they fear peers will think they are chicken if they don't. • Doesn't have confidence that they could get things by own effort.

ALCOHOL, OR OTHER DRUG PROBLEMS — misuses substances that could hurt self. • Afraid they won't have friends if they don't join others in drugs and drinking. • Thinks drugs are cool, tries to impress others with drug know-ledge or experience. • Uses the fact that many adults abuse drugs (such as alcohol) as an excuse for personal involvement in substance. • Can't really be happy without being high, or face problems without a crutch. • Acts as though he or she doesn't care about damaging or destroying self.

LYING — cannot be trusted to tell the truth. • Tells stories because he/she thinks others will like them better. • Likes to live in a make-believe, fantasy world. • Is afraid of having their mistakes discovered and so lies to cover-up. May even make up false problems to hide real ones. • Has told so many lies even when there is no apparent need to lie • Twists the truth to create a false impression but doesn't see this as lying.

FRONTING — puts on an act rather than having to show his/her real feelings to others — acts cool! • Always needs to appear big in the eyes of others, tries to prove themselves. • Bluffs and cons people, thinks loudness and slick talk are better than reason. • Acts superior, always has to be right, argues, needs to be best in everything, resents being beaten. • Clowns or shows off to get attention.

This list of behaviors comes from my **GROUP FACILITATION MANUAL,** created with Carla Chenoweth, a high school counselor who was instrumental in initiating over fifty-four skill-building groups of students in her school district. The booklet is an actual "how to set up and facilitate" any kind of support group of individuals, including adult groups, and helps to increase ones comfort level of security when they facilitate and not "control" or "fix" the group participants.

SLOW ISN'T BAD!
FAST ISN'T BETTER!
DIFFERENT ISN'T WRONG!

When we work with individuals we need to **respond** to them in an **esteeming** way. When we are out of esteem ourselves, our sense of **frustration** causes us to act out with behaviors that cause others to react against us.

In time this **defensiveness** causes both parties to not listen and to often hear what was not said. We all desire to be acknowledged and **appreciated** for our uniqueness so that we can better respect our differences.

Some of what we are dealing with in all this anger is the fact that for many people different is wrong.

In applying the technology in the program, **TRUE COLORS**™ created by Don Lowery, individuals have the chance to identify and list their joys and strengths as groups come together as allies celebrating behaviors and learning styles that make them unique. Listing the stresses and frustrations in our lives also affirms our diversity and uniqueness.

Universally within the four color groups of gold (responsible), green (analytical), blue (warm, caring) and orange (adventurous and often "at-risk") what stresses one group may be considered a positive attribute by another.

Since our attitude towards these differences is based on our conditioning from our environment, starting over with new choices and information permits us to reframe our views towards our peers and the rest of the world.

Life should be a vacation not just an event that happens a few weeks out of every year and after we retire. "When I retire, I can really get to where I want to be!" What a waste of human potential caused by choices we have made for ourselves that have lead us to believe that it was all we could have: "I will wait until later to enjoy life."

Celebrating our diversity allows us to enjoy life along the way to retirement. When we feel good about ourselves, we begin to feel good about others and become more accepting of our differences without judgment.

ACTIVITY #13: <u>Personal strengths</u>. Make a list of all the things you like about yourself. Who are you if you take away what you do? What do you value the most about yourself?

ACTIVITY #14: <u>Personal causes of stress and frustration</u>. Make a list of those things that cause you stress and frustration.

Which "color group," of gold (responsible), green (analytical), blue (warm, caring) and orange (adventurous and often "at-risk") do you place yourself? If you are within a group, identify with someone with your same strengths and frustrations. What did you discover?

ACTIVITY #15: **Issues of control and entrapment.** Can you really take charge of your life? Discuss within your group some of the things you learned, when you found yourself caught in these power struggles with different personalities that never seemed to resolve themselves. It is important to remember that different is just different. It is not right or wrong!

ACTIVITY #16: **Strategies for resolution of conflict.** Brainstorm some of the successful strategies you used to resolve conflict and not get hooked. Be proud of your strategies. It is our creativity that has provided you with the tools for survival in this sometimes difficult world. Please list below.

WHERE DO WE GO FROM HERE?

- IT'S ALL ABOUT HEALTHY CHOICES . . .

- IT'S ALL ABOUT FACING REALITY . . .

- IT'S ALL ABOUT FINDING A NETWORK OF SUPPORT <u>FOR YOURSELF</u> . . .

- IT'S ALL ABOUT <u>FORGIVENESS</u> OF YOURSELF FOR NOT KNOWING ANY BETTER . . .

- IT'S ALL ABOUT <u>FORGIVING OTHERS</u> . . .

- IT'S ALL ABOUT <u>LETTING GO OF</u> THE THINGS WE CANNOT <u>CONTROL</u> . . .

- IT'S ALL ABOUT <u>RELEASING THE NEGATIVE ENERGY</u> OF SELF-PITY THAT CREATES THE VICTIM IN US . .

- IT'S ALL ABOUT <u>TAKING CARE OF OURSELVES</u> AND BELIEVING THAT <u>WE DESERVE THAT CARE</u> . . .

- IT'S ALL ABOUT <u>CREATING A GOOD SELF-ESTEEM THROUGH POSITIVE SELF-AFFIRMATION</u> . . .

- IT'S ALL ABOUT <u>CHANGE</u> AND THAT <u>CHANGE BEGINS WITH US</u> . . .

If we wish to have good self-esteem then we must do our part to stop criticizing, complaining and fault-finding. These negative behaviors drain us of our energy. and **WE MUST STOP THE PUT DOWNS**. Replace these behaviors with positive thoughts and attitudes. It may be difficult at first. Fake it until you make it! With practice and a constant effort things will change.

BEGIN WITH YOURSELF: You cannot give what you do not have! Too often, we place so many conditions on our self-love, that we cannot see all the good things that are there. Learn to love yourself, unconditionally, without judgment.

ACTIVITY #17: The twenty-four hour challenge Challenge yourself and your friends to go 24 hours without a negative criticism or put down of anyone near you. *Begin one day at a time!*

It takes two people to have an argument. If one stops **"feeding fuel to the fire"** the fire will go out. The twenty-four hour challenge well heighten our awareness to not argue or put anyone down for one whole day. When we are too defensive and angry to hear what the other person is saying, we often argue only for the "adrenalin rush" that we have become use to during a fight or argument.

Begin each day by getting centered, focusing on the present moment and your purpose for being--- a teacher, parent, student, or whatever your job is at the moment. Being clear about your purpose, or goal, permits you to stay focused all day. It does not to allow the negativity around you to enter your mind and to wear you down.

Many of us do not realize how all these external issues rob us of our positive energy to do the job at hand. We need to replace the "concrete walls" around us that protect us, keeping others away, with "glass walls" that allow others to see us, as we really are, caring, loving and sensitive, but not allowing the negative messages to penetrate.

At this point a support person can be very valuable as you practice these new ways of responding to adversity or confrontation.

OUT WITTED
By Edwin Markham

Heretic, rebel, a thing to flout
He drew a circle that shut me out.
But love and I had the wit to win.
We drew a circle that took him in.

- CHAPTER 9 -

ACTION STRATEGIES

STRATEGY # 1

IDENTIFY THE PROBLEM
AND UNDERSTAND WHO OWNS IT!

Too often our co-dependency causes us to feel that the difficulties of others are some how partly our fault, and that it is our responsibility to "fix it" for them. This guilt or ownership, often connected to low self-esteem, can

- keep us from seeing who really has the problem,
- make us defensive to any form of suggestion or criticism,
- lead us to believe that everything that happens around us is our problem,
- weigh us down so low that we no longer have the energy to do anything.

STRATEGY # 2

SEPARATE FROM THE PROBLEM AND DO NOT OWN IT UNLESS YOU YOU ARE PART OF THE PROBLEM.

Sometimes we are the problem. We have all these expectations about how things should be or people should act, but nothing fits and no matter what we do nothing changes. We need to step back, take a breath, maybe even count to ten and let go of what we cannot change or control. This will release all that negative energy that locks us into conflict.

STRATEGY # 3

ACKNOWLEDGE THAT WE ARE POWERLESS OVER ANOTHER'S CHOICE OF BEHAVIOR.

We are. We just cannot be there all the time. We do, however, have tremendous power to choose our own boundaries, behaviors and attitudes.

We also have the right to choose what we will allow and what we will no longer allow in our lives.

NO ONE MAKES US DO ANYTHING!

- We can choose to behave a certain way.

- We can also choose the words that come from their mouth - good or bad.

- We can choose to argue or step back from the fight. Not to choose is also a choice!

STRATEGY # 4

LET GO OF WHAT WE CANNOT CONTROL. WE CAN ONLY CHANGE OURSELVES.

- Let go and release the bond of energy that locks the negative behavior in place.

- Try as we might to change others, they will make their own choices.

- The harder we try to control others the stronger will be their resistance to change and the more defensive they will become.

So often we are hooked into this negative cycle so tightly that we cannot see our choices.

We do have choices and we need to build on our strength and ability to make these choices to take care of ourselves.

STRATEGY # 5

SET CLEAR BOUNDARIES FOR
CERTAIN BEHAVIORS

- We need to be clear on what we will allow and what we will not allow in our lives and then stick to it.

- There may always be someone out there that wants to manipulate you into feeling that you are the crazy one.

- Stand firm on your decision to take care of yourself so you can better care for others.

STRATEGY # 6

PROVIDE REASONABLE, ACHIEVABLE
CONSEQUENCES FOR ANY
VIOLATION OF THOSE BOUNDARIES

You have every right to set boundaries and maintain your own space. At first others may not respect this because of your old behaviors, but when **"No!"** means **"No!"** and no longer means **"Maybe"** they will catch on, but probably not without some resistance at first. **Expect the resistance and pay close attention to your feelings** watching that you do not become defensive to their reaction to this new behavior of yours. It takes time to establish these new behaviors and to stick with them knowing you have a right to take care of yourself.

STRATEGY #7

FOLLOW THROUGH WITH THESE
CONSEQUENCES.

Stand firm on your commitment. There will be consequences from now on! This can be very difficult, especially if you have spent much of your life without boundaries.

YOU CREATE THEM AND STATE THEM
CLEARLY AND OFTEN!

It may surprise you that when your boundaries and limits are set clearly, after a while, they may back down and learn to live within those boundaries.

STRATEGY # 8

CHANGE YOUR REACTION TO THEIR
BEHAVIOR SO THAT THEY
MUST ALTER THEIR BEHAVIOR.

If your patterns for reacting change:

1. **Those** around you can no longer predict your behavior;

2. **They** will become confused and

3. **They** will be **"forced"** in a sense to look at their own behaviors and patterns.

How they feel about your choice to change is not your problem!

- **WE MUST TAKE CHARGE OF OUR OWN FEELINGS AND BEHAVIORS.**

- **WE MUST** REVIEW OUR STRATEGIES FOR SETTING BOUNDARIES.

- **WE MUST** STEP OFF OF THE ROLLER COASTER!

- **WE MUST** REALIZE THAT WE ARE NOT THE CRAZY ONES!

The "crazies" are caused by the negative cycle of trying to live behind a secret that controls us, as we pretend that everything is fine, fine, fine!

STRATEGY #9

WORK ON HEALTHY DETACHMENT WITH LOVE BY TAKING CARE OF YOURSELF.

---

1. Put up a **"glass wall"** to protect yourself from the negativity around you.

2. Accept others where they are at seeking out their good qualities and recognizing that they may never change.

3. Let go of the illusion of what could have been and accept the reality of what is.

4. In time observe if it is safe for you to remain in your circumstances, or if you might be better off getting some additional support.

5. Be open to the world around and begin to see the beauty that you may have missed due to the extensive negativity that has surrounded you in the past.

STRATEGY # 10

PRACTICE, PRACTICE, PRACTICE SO THAT THEY CAN NO LONGER PUSH YOUR BUTTONS.

A person wanting their independence needs to realize that they must take ownership and responsibility for the consequences of their choices and behaviors.
It takes time to learn this process, but it's worth the effort to regain your identity. Letting go of what we cannot control only makes us stronger as we unlock the power within ourselves that has been hidden.

With this new found energy we can now begin again to make healthy choices for ourselves as we realize that we have a right and an obligation to take care of ourselves.

As we begin to entertain only those thoughts and activities that will help us to remain healthy, our "stinkin' thinkin'" will become obvious to us. Some days we will take two steps forward and three steps back, but after some practice we will take six steps forward and only two steps back. Our personal growth and empowerment will all become very clear to us as we feel the new found energy that our successes will bring to us.

Who we are does not depend on what others think of us. Becoming an independent thinker can be quite a challenge for those who always sought the approval of others before they ever made a decision for themselves.

This is what it means to take the risk to change and to move beyond what was maybe thought to be safe and comfortable. As we begin to understand the real issue of co-dependency we will begin to see how it can be personally self-destructive. When we loose our identity, we also give up our personal power to make healthy choices for ourselves and we spend most of our time feeling trapped. It's all about choices and having the right to make those choices.

- CHAPTER 10 -

ISSUES OF CONTROL

Are we really as powerless as it seems to control the behavior of another individual? The answer is "YES!" especially if they are chemically dependent using a substance that has taken over their behavior, or toxic as children who can no longer feel, hear or trust because they have been poisoned by the dysfunctional behaviors of those around them.

"Control" has become an interesting word to define. So many of us desperately need to be in control, or we become scrambled, frightened and insecure. Others get the word "control" confused with the word "discipline."

We are working today with a new breed of young people trained and molded not only by their parents and churches, but, even more influentially, by the media. It has taught them that they are in control of their lives and that they have all the answers. As adolescents, at a point when they most need adults, they will choose to shut adults out and put up their walls. With this understanding, we need to find a common ground where young people can tell us their vision for themselves and not fear our judgment.

Unfortunately, our definition of control does not allow us to be vulnerable. Yet, that is exactly what we need to be. People in pain need us to be human with feelings, not some autocrat throwing out more rules and regulations. They must be given the chance to make rules for themselves.

Young people today know far more then we adults are willing to accept from them. Not only that, they have been asked to be adults at a very early age. Information overload and global competition have put tremendous pressure on them to succeed and make money. For some, this becomes a goal; others choose a different path. We can only help guide their choices— not make those choices for them.

TO LET GO TAKES LOVE

To "let go" does not mean to stop caring,
   it means I can't do it for someone else.
To "let go" is not to cut myself off,
   it is the realization I can't control another.

To "let go" is not to enable, but to allow
   learning from natural consequences.
To "let go" is to admit powerlessness which
   means the outcome is not in my hands.

To "let go" is not to try to change or blame
   another, it is to make the most of myself.
To "let go" is not to care for, but to care about.

To "let go" is not to fix , but to allow another
   to create solutions to their problems.
To "let go" is not to judge
   but to allow another to be a human being.

To "let go" is not to be in the middle arranging all
   the outcomes, but to allow others to affect
   their own destinies.
To "let go" is not to be protective,
   it is to permit another to face reality

To "let go" is not to deny, but to accept.
To "let go" is not to nag, scold, or argue, but to
   search out my own shortcomings and
   correct them.

To "let go" is not to criticize and regulate
   anybody but to try to become what I dream I
   can be.
To "let go" is not to regret the past,
   but to grow and to live for the future.

To "let go" is to fear less and to love more.

Anonymous

DO YOU EMPOWER, AS A HELPER, OR ENABLE, AS ONE WHO CONTROLS?

ENABLERS do things for people they are trying to help and lock them into the behaviors that they wish they would change.

> **PEOPLE WHO EMPOWER** are just there for others and change their reactions to the uncomfortable behavior with gentleness.

ENABLERS try to dominate and control to change the actions of others.

> **PEOPLE WHO EMPOWER** let go of control and let life happen seeking to change only the things they can change and seek the wisdom the know the difference.

ENABLERS become exhausted mulling over the past with regret or trying to find ways to escape a future that has not yet arrived.

> **PEOPLE WHO EMPOWER** choose where they will use their energy and spend their time living for today.

ENABLERS tend to convert their frustrations into negativity, fear and contempt for what others do and do not do and have difficulty respecting the individuality of others.

> **PEOPLE WHO EMPOWER** approach others with a positive attitude, being open and willing to listen to another point of view.

ENABLERS often get hostile, and manipulative when others don't fulfill their expectations.

> **PEOPLE WHO EMPOWER** release others with love and do not try to fit them into a standard or preformed image.

"Does Anyone Hear Our Cries For Help?" by Bertie Synowiec

ENABLERS stifle the growth of individuals by always telling them what to do and not allowing them to think for themselves and learn from their mistakes.

PEOPLE WHO EMPOWER give others the opportunity to pursue their own destiny, regardless of their choices.

ENABLERS panic first and think it through later burning all their energy until they become immobile and incapable of doing anything.

PEOPLE WHO EMPOWER enjoy the peacefulness of their serenity and concentrate their energy on their own personal growth.

ENABLERS blame others for what then don't understand and wallow in self-pity trying to solve their problems by changing the world.

PEOPLE WHO EMPOWER work on understanding themselves as part of the problem.

ENABLERS spend their time being disappointed that their unrealistic expectations of others are never fulfilled.

PEOPLE WHO EMPOWER drop all expectations for others and accept them unconditionally without judgment.

ENABLERS judge people on what they think they know, failing to realize that there is so much that they do not know.

PEOPLE WHO EMPOWER give others credit for attempts at change and frespect the privacy of others.

ENABLERS create illusions of what their world should be and strive to place everyone into a particular category that meets their needs.

PEOPLE WHO EMPOWER let go of the illusion of what could have been and live in the reality of the present moment letting each day unravel.

ENABLERS consume all their energy trying to change the world.

PEOPLE WHO EMPOWER choose the path towards self-improvement. They know that they can only change themselves and that others they can only love.

> Do not feel totally, personally, irrevocably, responsible for everything. That is my job.
> God

WHOSE JOB IS IT?

This is a story about four people named Everybody, Somebody, Anybody, and Nobody.

There was an important job to be done and Everybody was asked to do it.

Everybody was sure Somebody would do it. Anybody could have done it, but Nobody did it.

Somebody got angry about that, because it was Everybody's job.

Everybody thought Anybody could do it, but Nobody realized that Everybody wouldn't do it.

It ended up that Everybody blamed Somebody when Nobody did what Anybody could have done.

Author unknown

Page for Notes

"Does Anyone Hear Our Cries For Help?" by Bertie Synowiec

- CHAPTER 11 -

PROBLEM OWNERSHIP

Sometimes, as adults, and young people, we know too much about the consequences of someone else's behavior and we take over, and their problem becomes our problem. We just cannot separate from it. We so desperately want to prevent them from making any mistakes that we totally lose site of our purpose and responsibility.

As we try to step back and look at the issue of problem ownership, I would like to use the example of a young person going off to college.

We adults sure do know what is out there for them. We hope that we have given them the tools and good sense to deal with difficult situations, and the knowledge to stay clear of those things they should not mess with. In reality, no matter what we do, they will make their own choices. To ease our fear and ownership of their mistakes, we might remind them, that if they are responsible enough to make certain choices for themselves, then they must also be responsible enough to take responsibility for the consequences of their behaviors.

Understanding problem ownership can be very liberating for co-dependents who have spent their life looking out for the well-being of others. Those who have difficulty identifying the problem may choose to use the following model to see who owns it.

PROBLEM SOLVING MODEL

1. ### STATE THE PROBLEM
   . . . "My father is a alcoholic." . . . "My parents are divorced."
   . . . "I'm failing my classes and I won't graduate."

2. EXPRESS HOW YOU FEEL
... "I feel afraid." ... "I'm scared."
... "I feel ashamed."

3. SPEAK TO A COMPETENT AND TRUSTWORTHY ADULT
... who will listen to you and not judge you
... who will let you talk your feelings out

4. FIND A SUPPORT GROUP THAT SHARES SIMILAR PROBLEMS
... ask some significant, trustworthy adult for help in starting this group, or direction to where you may join an existing group

5. KNOW THAT THE ONLY PERSON YOU CAN "WORK ON" IS YOU
... I can't change what my parents are doing.
... I can't change my brothers and sisters. .. I can ask myself -
   ... what can I do to help the situation?
   ... do I waste time worrying about things I can't fix?
   ... am I willing to accept responsibility for my life?

Author unknown

PROBLEM SOLVING METHODS

1. **NEGOTIATING** — students talk about their position in the conflict and discuss what might be done about it.

2. **COMPROMISING** — both parties give up something to resolve conflict.

3. **TAKING TURNS** — one individual goes first and the other second.

"Does Anyone Hear Our Cries For Help?" by Bertie Synowiec

4. **ACTIVE LISTENING** — perceiving what the other individual is saying and also feeding it back accurately.

5. **THREAT-FREE EXPLANATION** — an individual communicates his/her position in a conflict without threatening the other person.

6. **APOLOGIZING**— saying you're sorry without saying you're wrong.

7. **SOLICITING INTERVENTION** — seeking consultation or help when the issue is too complex, or "heavy" to handle.

8. **POSTPONING** — individuals agree to wait for a more appropriate time to handle the situation.

9. **DISTRACTING** — calling attention to something away from the conflict.

10. **ABANDONING** — moving away from situation that cannot be dealt with.

11. **EXAGGERATING** — role playing an exaggerated interpretation of issue.

12. **HUMOR** — the angry feelings associated with conflict are diffused in some humorous and constructive way.

13. **CHANCE** — a technique such as flipping a coin, is used to decide a conflict.

14. **SHARING** — the individuals decide to share for the benefit of both.

NOTE: The above 14 strategies are considered to be primarily positive. The following have negative consequences and their use should be discouraged.

15. **VIOLENCE** — verbal or physical abuse used to deal with conflict.

16. **FLIGHT** — an individual retreats internally or physically, leaving a conflict when he/she should have worked it through.
17. **MANIPULATION** — an individual attempts to enlist others to handle conflicts for him instead of taking responsibility. Give a person a fish and they'll eat for a day. Teach him/her how to fish and they will eat for life.

TEN COMMANDMENTS OF GOOD LISTENING

1. **STOP TALKING!** You cannot listen if you are talking. Wait, your turn will come.
2. **PUT THE TALKER AT EASE.** Help him/her feel that they are free to talk. This is often called a "permissive, safe environment."
3. **SHOW HIM/HER THAT YOU WANT TO LISTEN.** Look and act interested. Listen to understand, rather than to reply.
4. **REMOVE DISTRACTIONS.** Don't doodle, tap, read, or shuffle papers. Will it be quieter if you shut the door or turn down the radio?
5. **EMPATHIZE WITH HIM/HER.** Try to put yourself in his/her place so that you can see their point of view.
6. **BE PATIENT.** Allow plenty of time. Don't interrupt. Don't start for the door, or walk away, or make hand signals to hurry them along.
7. **HOLD YOUR TEMPER.** An angry person gets the wrong meaning from words and the anger inhibits active listening.
8. **GO EASY ON ARGUMENT AND CRITICISM.** This puts the talker on the defensive. He/she may "clam up" and get angry.
9. **ASK QUESTIONS.** This encourages the expansion of their thoughts and shows you are listening and helps them to develop points further.
10. **STOP TALKING!** You just can't do a good job of listening while you are talking.

Author unknown

LISTEN

When I ask you to listen to me and you start giving advice, you have not done what I ask. When I ask you to listen to me and you begin to tell me why I should not feel that way, you have trapped my feelings.

When I ask you to listen to me and you feel you have to do something to solve my problem, you have failed me, strange as that may seem.

Listen! All I ask, is that you listen, not talk or do but just listen and hear me. Advice is cheap. Twenty-five cents will get you both Dear Abby and Billy Graham in the newspaper. I can do for myself! I am not helpless. Maybe discouraged and faltering, but not helpless.

When you do something for me that I can do for myself, you contribute to my fear and weakness; but when you accept as a simple fact that I do feel what I feel, no matter how irrational, then I can quit trying to convince you and get about the business of understanding what's behind this irrational feeling, and when it's clear, the answers are obvious and I don't need advice.

Irrational feelings make sense when we understand them. Perhaps that is why prayer works sometimes for some people because God is mute and he doesn't give advice or try to fix things. He just listens and lets you work it out for yourself.

So please, listen and just hear me. If you want to talk, wait a minute for your turn and I'll listen to you.

Anonymous

Nature gave us two ears, but only one tongue, which is a gentle reminder that we should listen more than we talk!

Page for Notes

- CHAPTER 12 -

SETTING BOUNDARIES

Setting boundaries is directly related to the choices we give to others to be responsible for their behavior and the consequences of that behavior. It then becomes their problem to fix, not yours.

When we reach the point where everyone seems to be taking advantage of our good nature and we have little, or no time, to take care of ourselves, we will be desperate enough to set boundaries. We just need to make it clear that certain behaviors, whatever they are, will no longer be acceptable. If we make it uncomfortable enough for them to behave a certain way because of the consequences, they must choose to leave, or change.

This works with both young people and adults. It is risky and we are not always ready to take these risks that require us to change. Our self-esteem may just be too fragile. Often times the behavior that follows the changes is very confusing. It is new behavior, and often the reaction to it will be angry behavior. By changing our reaction to their behavior, people become nervous and can no longer predict the outcome.

At this point, we may need the support of another individual who "speaks our language," as we look for the strength to stand firm on what we need for ourselves in order to survive and be all we were meant to be. If you are serious about learning more, Al-anon and Families Anonymous are wonderful support groups. Their meeting dates can be found by calling your local Alcohol Anonymous Group listed in the phone book. You may also create your own circle of friends to help you get started.

We all have much to learn, if we will only take the risk to begin the process. Whose job is it anyway to take care of **ME**?

WE NO LONGER DANCED HER DANCE

She "God-damned this!" and "God-damned that!"
We held the line and stated the facts.
We no longer danced her dance.

"You'll bury me first before meals on wheels"
That may just happen, unless she yields.
We no longer danced her dance.

"Nobody loves me, nobody cares."
We paid the bills, and tended to her affairs.
We no longer danced her dance.

The abuse she gave, the abuse we took.
The pain runs deep! We took a look.
We no longer danced her dance.

The car is gone, the keys are away.
You think it's fun being your parent for a day?
We no longer danced her dance.

A little voice sixty years your pleaser,
Asks, "Why can't we help make their lives a little easier?"
He can no longer dance your dance.

Our energy is drained. We need to go on.
Your choices are clear, the last dance has gone.
We'll no longer dance your dance.

©1991 Bertie Ryan Synowiec

CREATING A CONSISTENT PLAN OF ACTION

Individuals choose their behaviors, good or bad, to fulfill a need to belong. They act out to gain attention, to feel powerful, or revengeful, or to avoid failure. When people feel that there is a place for them where they can be successful and can contribute to the group in a positive way, they no longer have to "act out" to fulfill this need to belong.

These behaviors must be identified and described clearly, with all parties listening carefully. Too often the causes, motives, goals and consequences for a certain behavior are not clear and the disciplinarian will react to what they think the situation is, rather then what actually happened. Intervention must be spontaneous and consistent, appropriately fitting the action that has caused the disruption.

What this means is that, for example, when individuals act out and want recognition, the "time out room" experience would give them a chance to re-think the motive behind their behavior. This form of discipline would not "fit" the person who was trying to avoid failure, or who did not complete their job assignment and wanted to escape to a place where they could be alone.

1. **DESCRIBE THE BEHAVIOR OBJECTIVELY**. Be careful not to get your own "stuff" subjectively in the way.

2. **IDENTIFY THE GOAL OF THE BEHAVIOR:** Attention, power, control, insecurity, fear of something new, issues of change etc.

3. **CHOOSE THE APPROPRIATE INTERVENTION STRATEGY:**

   • Ignore the behavior or give them the "eye." Stand near, or signal to them silently with a predetermined signal.

- Create an example from the behavior. Have everyone join in the behavior such as, "tapping their pencils."

- Be patient and allow a certain amount of misbehavior while the individual learns to control these behavior. Agree to this ahead of time!

- Surprise the individual with an unexpected positive reaction.

- Distract the person with gentle direct questions.

- Catch them being good. Thank them.

- Change the person's desk or work station. Move them to a special quiet place.

4. **ENCOURAGE THE USE OF SELF-ESTEEM BUILDERS:**

- Reduce hostility and build positive relationships by helping individuals express feelings without fear of criticism or rejection.

- If they are fearful of failure you may wish to modify your your approach towards them to encourage more success.

- Provide additional support durings the training period or learning process to build self-confidence with positive affirmation.

- Remember to celebrate diversity and uniqueness. Everyone has their own best way to learn something. Allow time to understand their learning style.

- CHAPTER 13 -

TEACHER/PARENT/STUDENT RELATIONSHIPS

STRATEGIES FOR BUILDING PARTNERSHIPS

1. Acknowledge the parent as the authority on their child. Ask them to teach you the things you need to know about their child so that you both may work better together. Encourage them to become advocates for their child and not be threatened when someone doubts their beliefs. Certain emotional and academic handicaps just cannot be seen by certain teachers who believe their job is only to teach. Help them to understand that things are changing and we are learning to teach to the whole child.

2. Recognize that often the parent may feel intimidated in the presence of a teacher. Maybe they did not do well in school, or had other bad experiences relating to their education that caused them to drop out of school. Understand that their underlying fear of the teacher may be caused by the "secrets" that they are guarding, and that they may feel that the situation caused in the classroom by their child may be their fault and could have been prevented, if they had been a better parent.

3. Trust that the parent, or parents, may also be at their "wits end" with the behavior of their child due to lack of understanding. If their child, or spouse, is abusing alcohol or other drugs, they may believe that "they are the crazy one" and unable to express anything right since everything is so unmanageable. Using some parallel example's begin to help them to see the universality of their feelings and the behavior of their child. You might explain how Families Anonymous, may help them find the support they need to take care of themselves.

4. Realize that parents with attention deficit, special education children often live with the same condition in themselves and look at it as normal behavior. Recognize also that these parents have suffered in their educational training because they, too, did not fit into the left-brained organized linear system. Their self-esteem is fragile, but their detemination to make it better for their child is not. Become a good listener and be careful not to become defensive to their anger. They are angry at the system and at their inability to control what is happening. They are not angry at you.

5. Invite the child and parent to be involved in the educational plan of their child. Create a portfolio of their best accomplishments so that, when they graduate, they will have the skills to get a job that meets their needs and fits their goals as a student. Meet with parents at least twice a year to discuss the good things their child is doing in your classroom. Their child is more than just a grade in the grade book. He or she is a person with many talents and some of these talents do not get graded in school. Ask parents about what he or she does, successfully, at other times.

INVOLVE PARENTS IN PARTNERSHIPS

• Parents are experts in understanding the behavior of their child. Some may be defensive due to their own low self-esteem and frustration.

• Encourage them to be part of their child's academic growth and be careful not to put them on the spot. Some may be blaming their child's difficulties on their own inability to cope with a difficult situation at home that they guard as a "secret."

• Provide information for parents with work-shops and programs that can get them involved comfortably.

- Encourage support group participation, such as Families Anonymous or Al-anon, for families in crisis so that they may realize that they are not alone and can grow with this new found support.

- Understand that you need their support and they need yours in the education of their child. Help them to know that they can ask for this.

THINGS TO REMEMBER:

- **Avoid confrontation, physical, verbal and psychological attacks**. You need not own their problem or lack of understanding.

- **Be careful not to diminish legitimate power.** Help individuals understand what is age appropriate. Some children come from homes where they are the adult! Acknowledge this when necessary.

- **Remember that hurting people hurt people.** Revenge can be cruel. Most people are just protecting themselves from further hurts.

- **Avoid labels.** Separate the bad behavior from the good person. Be consistent, firm and friendly and have reasonable behavioral expectations.

- **Be careful not to become part of the problem!** Model the behavior you expect from others and always show respect.

- **Be clear on the consequences.** Allow for restitution and repair of damage in whatever form.

STEPS TO BETTER UNDERSTAND
INDIVIDUALS THAT LEARN DIFFERENTY

- Give them unconditional love and support.
- Believe your instincts. Become their advocate.
- Never give up and cry with them.
- Work through your frustrations and acknowlege them.
- Understand that hurting people hurt people, especially those feeling abused.
- Mistakes of the past were only opportunities to learn. Stay in the present time.
- Help them set goals and allow for creativity everywhere even in a mess.
- Motivate, motivate, motivate by only pointing out their positive actions.
- Stay close, but do not smother. Empower them to learn for themselves.
- Teach them to become a <u>Pro at Hard Work</u>.
- Believe in their power and intelligence, not their grades.
- Let go of expectations and forced time lines attached to old standards.
- Appreciate their way of doing things and their learning style.
- Build self-esteem through small successes that will later become greater.
- Affirm what they feel and see. Understand their uniqueness.
- Understand abuse in all its forms. Violence in any form is never allowed!
- Since you can not change difficult people, change your attitude towards them.
- Teach them problem ownership and healthy detachment from the things they can not change: such as, put downs, negativitity and teasing.
- Be responsible for yourself and your own honesty and integrity.
- Always model the kind of behavior and respect you want from others.
- Recognize growth and change. Trust them and teach them to be trustworthy.
- Model for them a "no use" alcohol/drug message.

90   "Does Anyone Hear Our Cries For Help?" by Bertie Synowiec

Their brain cells are counted!

- Allow them to get high on life and on their own feelings of accomplishments.
- Learn about alcohol abuse, personality changes and denial. "Not my kid!"
- Understand the family system and share your fears and concerns with a friend.
- Set boundaries and clear limits. Keep acceptable behaviors within them.
- Stand firm on consequences for inappropriate behaviors.
- Let go of the judgments of others. Do what is right for you.
- Learn lessons that value positive ideals with activities outside of school.
- Help them experience learning outside of books as motivation to read.
- Teach them typing, the use of the computer, spell-check and the calculator.
- Encourage band, sports and other hands-on activities.
- Say "yes" more than "no." "If we had ever said never, I never would have learned those spelling words," a student once cautioned his mother!
- Write out achievable goals and review often. Place in wallet or other safe place.
- Teach leadership everyday and model it for them. They know the difference!
- Understand and accept your own learning disabilities. Build on their individuality.
- Work hard on your own feelings of intimidation or sense of failure.
- Model good self-esteem. Your children may reflect your behaviors, but they are not you.
- Encourage other siblings, that can, to help with tutoring and extra support.
- Avoid the resistors or those with an agenda for your child beyond their capability.
- Trust your child's resiliency to survive and develop their own coping skills.
- Believe in your child. Love them unconditionally. Work closely with their teachers and their school.

WHEN YOUR BEST IS GOOD ENOUGH
by Barbara Ryan Larkin

A baby is born and lives are changed, the script is
new and rearranged.
Each phrase, each step is watched with care,
The stats are checked and we compare
Our infant, toddler, child with the rest.
When school begins, we want the best. Are you
reading yet?
Are you first, or last? Are you keeping up with the
rest of the class?

Are you doing your best? Can you do better than
that?
Could you hurry please? What **LEVEL** are you at?
I have plans for you, you have to fit. If something is
wrong, can I deal with it?
You've worked, you're slow, it's becoming clear,
Your best is okay, but not quite near what I thought
your best would be.
Do you feel that you've disappointed me?

It's time to stop, to think this through, I only want
what's best for you.
The problem lies, it's plain to see, not with you, but
clearly with me.
You're happy and growing at your own pace,
I guess I thought you'd be in first place.
But so did many others say,
Their child would come in first some day.

So as I see you growing strong,
I realize who you are, and that I've been wrong.
What's wrong is what's inside of me, that I haven't
allowed you to just be
Who you are, at this point in time,
And let you grow on your own time line
You've done your best to grow so free.

And I loved you, and helped you to see the world as I
saw it, right or wrong, And without me now you'll
move along.

I'd like to think when I'm old and grey,
And all those school papers are tucked away,
You'll sit with your children and tell them true,
How your parents struggled raising you.

I'll have taught you, I hope, that life just takes place,
To learn the joy in just running the race.
You'll tell your children in honesty,
If you happened to "win" it was meant to be.

Please pass on to your child these messages too,
That I loved you most when I accepted you.
When I let your best satisfy me,
Regardless of what level you turned out to be.
And remember, as your parent, I struggled too,
But I always gave my best to you.

©1991 Barbara Ryan Larkin

I'M A PRO AT HARD WORK

PERFECT PEOPLE... PERFECT ADULTS... PERFECT CHILDREN... All of them "A" students... All of them overachievers... All of them perfect little people... All of them making us big people look good. All of them succeeding in the things we adults never would have tried. All of them measuring their success as a person by the "A" grades they get in school. **ALL OF THEM PERFECT... PERFECT... PERFECT...** No time to play... Must study, study, study... No time to relate... Must study, study, study... Grades, grades, grades... That's what's important... That's what gets you into college... That's what makes you successful... So what if you're not flexible...
  PERFECT... PERFECT... PERFECT... THAT'S WHAT COUNTS... So they have all "A" 's... How well will they deal with the everyday real world of imperfection? Will they ever know how to give out a compliment, or a word of encouragement to those who are trying their best? Will they ever see the positives?
  WILL THEY KNOW HOW TO DO WHAT DOESN"T COME OUT OF A BOOK?

- Have they ever built a tree fort from salvaged wood scraps? Can they sail a 30 foot boat at winning speed?
- Can they design, rig and build their own sail boat, bowsprit and all and sew it's sails and shamrock burgee?
- Can they figure out how to exchange a new trailer from under a nine hundred pound boat without putting it in the water.
- Can they change the oil in a car, van, or truck, or change a tire on a major highway? Or put up a 4' by 8' wall, studs, sheet rock and all.
- Have they ever taken mirror squares and cut them into one inch squares, to build a mirror ball?
- Have they ever run cross country for two hours and played football for two hours on the same night for three months?
- Created their own stencil to paint on a tee-shirt? Tie-dyed their own designer's original?
- Organized a band of fourteen eleven-year-olds to play at a peanut bowl game, or sang a solo on opening night? Organized group ski days at Mount Trashmore so friends could have something to do?
- Climbed the sides of rocky cliffs, as if their feet had glue on their bottoms, and dove from thirty feet in the air into the lake?

He had done all these things by the time he was twelve, but based on his grades, he was not the perfect student. He was not a perfect person! He did not get the "A" grade... He could read into your heart and could tell when you were sad, or troubled, and ask, "Are you okay?" But he was not the perfect "A"... Gifted?? He was more gifted than most kids... He just has difficulty reading and was never going to let it stop him! You see, **HE'S A PRO AT HARD WORK** and is always willing to try new things, fearlessly... With that, what other tools in life does he need? **HE'S OUR "C" STUDENT AND FOR US - THAT'S PERFECT!!**

©1989 Bertie Ryan Synowiec

BUIILDING POSITIVE RELATIONSHIPS
WITH YOUR CHILD

- **THE 24-HOUR CHALLENGE** - Challenge friends, family or co-workers to go without a single put down or negative criticism for twenty-four hours. If anyone messes up, they must start again until they reach 24 hours of peacefullness.

- **LISTEN TO YOUR CHILD** - Ask questions about their feelings rather than give advice. "Why did someone make you angry?" "How do you like the way you decorated your room?"

- **PRAISE BEHAVIOR WHEN YOU GIVE THEM COMPLIMENTS** - Look for good behavior reinforcing it with positive statements. Teach them the difference between who they are and what they do. Children need to feel valued for just being-- apart from their activities.

- **POSITIVELY DEAL WITH FAILURE** - We need not dwell on the causes for failure. We learn from our mistakes and move onto more positive behavior. The mistake does not make the child a bad person. Separate the two.

- **BE SENSITIVE TO BIG HURTS** like rejection, exclusion, betrayal, disillusionment and loneliness. Really be there. They need not talk about it. Just let them know you love them and will support them.

- **TOO MUCH PRESSURE ON CHILDREN** causes them to think they can never please anyone. Small achievements need to be recognized as the stepping stones to greater successes.

- **PRACTICE ACCEPTANCE AND UNDER-STANDING** - Kids often test their parents with only half of the story. They must feel safe to share more deeply. If we get angry, they will clam up fearing rejection or being hurt.

95   "Does Anyone Hear Our Cries For Help?" by Bertie Synowiec

- **BE REAL TO YOUR CHILDREN** - Remember your own early years when you felt scared, smothered, hurt, rejected or embarrassed. Share these feelings and memories with your children. Be honest and non-judgmental.

- **SET GUIDELINES FOR RESPONSIBILITIES** - Focus on the issue and not the emotion. Feelings are neither right or wrong; they are just feelings. Try not to let your fears cloud your ability to be sensitive and understanding.

- **GIVE THEM CHOICES AND PERMIT THEM TO MAKE THEIR OWN DECISIONS** - Explain your feelings of concern. Then, let them choose their clothes, or if they will study early or late, etc.

- **DIG DEEP WITHIN YOURSELF FOR UNDERSTANDING AND PATIENCE** - We don't always remember that they, too, are trying to sort out their lives with so many changes happening all at once, both emotional and physical.

- **GIVE THEM YOUR TIME** - This is a very precious gift that you both can share and can only result in better communication and understanding.

A BILL OF RIGHTS FOR
KIDS OF DIVORCED PARENTS

1. **THE RIGHT TO BE TREATED AS IMPORTANT HUMAN BEINGS**, with unique feelings, ideas and desires and not as a source of argument between parents.

2. **THE RIGHT TO A CONTINUING RELATIONSHIP WITH BOTH PARENTS** and the freedom to receive love from and express love for both.

3. THE RIGHT TO EXPRESS LOVE AND AFFECTION FOR EACH PARENT without having to stifle that love because of fear of disapproval by the other parent.

4. THE RIGHT TO KNOW THAT THEIR PARENTS' DECISION TO DIVORCE IS NOT THE RESPONSIBILITY OF THE CHILD and that they will live with one parent and will visit the other parent.

5. THE RIGHT TO CONTINUING CARE and guidance from both parents.

6. THE RIGHT TO HONEST ANSWERS TO QUESTIONS about the changing family relations.

7. THE RIGHT TO KNOW AND APPRECIATE WHAT IS GOOD IN EACH PARENT without one parent degrading the other.

8. THE RIGHT TO HAVE A RELAXED, SECURE RELATIONSHIP with both parents without being placed in a position to manipulate one parent against the other.

9. THE RIGHT TO HAVE THE CUSTODIAL PARENT NOT UNDERMINE VISITATION by suggesting tempting alternatives, or by threatening to withhold visitation as a punishment for a wrong.

10. THE RIGHT TO EXPERIENCE REGULAR AND CONSISTENT VISITATION and the right to know the reason for a cancelled visit.

Author Unknown

ADOLESCENTS NEED. . . .

- **LIMITS SET** - They need to know what is acceptable and what is not. What are the consequences? No second chances. Eliminate the gray areas so that they know their limitations.

- **DISCIPLINE** - Should be consistent and fair and not reactive to your own issues. This should be applied to all areas of their lives.

- **POSITIVE ROLE MODELS** - How do we adults handle stress, celebration, and our social life?

- **HONEST EXPRESSION** - Adolescents need a place that is safe for them to open up and share their feelings and thoughts.

- **PERMISSION TO FAIL AND RETURN** - Adolescents learn from their mistakes; we need not accept the misbehavior, but we must accept the child. Mistakes need not mean that the child is a bad person.

- **LAUGHTER** - Adolescents need an opportunity to laugh and to have fun.

- **SUCCESS** - They need an opportunity to be successful in school, at home, in the community and with their peers. **ENCOURAGE THEM!**

- **STRUCTURED FAMILY ACTIVITIES** - meals, meals, outings, riding in the same car to activities.

- **CONSISTENCY** - This is lacking everywhere - with friends, school policy, parents, rules and regulations in general.

- **ACCURATE INFORMATION ABOUT DRUGS AND ALCOHOL** - plus crime, sexuality and other areas that might promote **FEAR**.

- **COMMUNICATION WITH ADULTS AND PARENTS** - They need this and we adults need this to reduce our fears.

- **SUPPORT FROM IMPORTANT ADULTS AND FROM THEIR PEERS** - Its tough to grow up alone without this support.

- **TO BE TRUSTED BY IMPORTANT ADULTS** - This builds their self-confidence and makes them trustworthy.

- **GENUINE COMMITMENT FROM FAMILY AND FRIENDS** - They need the sense that they belong.

- **BE ENCOURAGED TO BE RESPONSIBLE** - They need to feel that other people can count on them when they need to count on them.

- **TO BE RESPECTED** - so that they will respect others. You can't give what you don't have.

- **TO BE TOUCHED** - It is incredible that we need a bumper sticker to remind us to hug our kids today.

- **UNCONDITIONAL LOVE** - They need to be told that you love them, not just when they are good but always.

- **A HIGHER POWER** - As Alchoholics Anonymous calls it. It is a power within themselves, greater than themselves to whom they can pray and ask for help when all else fails.

- **YOU** - They need you. Take the time to listen and be there for them.

Author Unknown

Page for Notes

"Does Anyone Hear Our Cries For Help?" by Bertie Synowiec

- CHAPTER 14 -

STAGES OF FORGIVENESS: ISSUES OF ANGER

Adapted from **Suzanne and Sidney Simon's book: "FORGIVENESS - How to make peace with your past and get on with your life."** Published by Warner Books, Inc. 1990 and available through Values Associates, 45 Old Mountain Road, Hadley, MA 01035. Used with permission.

The following process is based on forgiving ourselves, or another, for perhaps, what we, or they, did not know or understand. Forgiveness creates an opportunity for individuals to release that negative energy that keeps them locked in place. Understanding and acting upon the following stages will help us to let go of the control these issues have had on our lives.

STAGE I - DENIAL

"It's not that bad; others have had it worse." "It never happened to me." We have occluded the memory of the situation. Children who are battered forget their childhood. They can't handle the thought of seeing themselves as damaged goods.

Siblings in an Alcoholic home seldom share their feelings with one another. Feelings don't count. "If I don't feel then maybe it didn't happen." They don't trust and they don't speak as long as there is a secret to guard.

Letting go of the illusion that we have created to protect us from seeing the pain will help us to face the reality of our present situation. Denial locks us in place and prevents us from moving forward. Making lists, as in the following exercise, will help us take the first step towards forgiveness as we become more objective to our situation.

ACTIVITY #18: Hurting People hurt people.

Make a list of people who have hurt you in one column and in the other column list the people in your life that you have hurt. You may wish to indicate how you have been hurt and how you hurt them.

PEOPLE THAT HAVE HURT ME	PERSONS THAT I HAVE HURT

Take a look at these lists carefully and realize that sometimes we become stuck in all that negative energy because we can not let go of the pain, guilt and fear connected with that sense of powerlessness we felt when we were being hurt. We were never really powerless. We just had not yet discovered the source of our personal power.

Look also at the people in our lives that we have hurt for whatever reason. Perhaps we were hurting so much at the time that we were only trying to survive. Hurting people hurt people. This may be a very tender moment and we are not to pass judgment on ourselves or others at this time. Be sure to acknowledge the exact nature of our wrongs and those of others so that we are clear as to what action steps we need to take as we move on.

Doing this personal inventory of ourselves will help us to see our imperfections and that, at times, because of our negativity and pain we become part of the problem. This prevents us from getting any closure on these issues. As we begin to identify what we previously could not look at, we may find ourselves taking on all the blame for what had occurred for whatever reason. This leads us into the next stage. *(Adapted from Suzanne and Sidney Simon's book: FORGIVENESS - Warner Books 1990. Used with permission.)*

STAGE II - SELF-BLAME

When we are in this stage we feel that we set it up; "I asked for it; it was my fault; if I only had..." Adult Children of Alcoholics feel that if only they had hidden the bottle, cleaned the house, did their homework, were more perfect! People stuck in self-blame are blaming themselves unmercifully. If we don't deal with it, it will not go away. If we keep shoving it down, it will keep coming back. Some things were just not our fault.

Look at your list above again and begin to separate what you could control from what you could not control in your life. Separate what you did - the list on the right - from what was done to you. When the distinction becomes clear to you, then you may begin to see yourself as a victim. Many people spend too much time, sometime years, in the victim stage. So much personal destruction takes place as we sit, wasting time and energy feeling sorry for ourselves, pulling everyone into our self-pity.

STAGE III - VICTIM

Victims beget victims. As this stage drains us of our energy and gives us an eventual sense of complete powerlessness, we begin to seek a support group of individuals with similar feelings to help sort this out. We begin to see that something is definitely wrong in our lives. Our tears come from all the years we stuffed our feelings. Its okay to let them come.

Unless we become what is called a cycle-breaker, the cycle will continue and nothing will change. We must admit that we are a victim of whatever: physical abuse, incest, divorce, alcohol abuse, etc. and stop blaming ourselves. We need to mourn and grieve over the loss of what could have been had things been different and let go of the illusion of what never was. Facing the reality of our lives may force us to make decisions to change our attitude towards our offender.

(Adapted from Suzanne and Sidney Simon's book: FORGIVENESS - Warner Books 1990. Used with permission.)

None of us deserved the bad treatment we got. As long as we blame ourselves, and as long as we refuse to say this person made mistakes, we will remain a victim and no change will occur. Chances are that they did the best that they knew how, but what they did was wrong and we must admit that. The healing process takes time. If we are not willing to do the work, the pain will not go away. We need support and encouragement to process this and move away from the pain. I must give attention to myself.

ACTIVITY #19: Issues affecting those that have hurt you. Look at the names on your list of people who have hurt you. Take one of the names and make a list of the things that have fed into his or her life when he or she was growing up. On the opposite column make a list of the things that have fed into your life that may have caused you to justify your behavior towards the person that you have hurt.

ISSUES IN THEIR LIVES PEOPLE THAT HAVE HURT ME	ISSUES IN MY LIFE PEOPLE THAT I HAVE HURT

Take a look at these lists carefully, and objectively see if the circumstances in the lives of these individuals may have given them permission to behave in a way that was, perhaps, modeled for them by their parents or family. As you do this exercise, you may begin to feel yourself moving away from feeling sorry for yourself as a victim and into the next stage becoming angry and indignant.

(Adapted from Suzanne and Sidney Simon's book: FORGIVENESS Warner Books1990. Used with permission.)

STAGE IV - INDIGNATION

Righteous anger: "No one should treat anyone the way I was treated." This anger can eat at us making us generalize: "All men/women are..." or "All husbands/wives are..." a certain way. We get angry at all men, or all women, for example.

We need to feel how wrong the behavior was and process this anger and then let go of it. Is it serving you well to keep up the rage? Is it worth spending all your positive energy in such a negative direction? How long will we keep punishing them for hurting us?

Letting go as we pass through this stage and releasing this negative energy will help us to begin to see the circumstances and the individuals involved in a different light. They will no longer be able to consume our time and energy.

(Adapted from Suzanne and Sidney Simon's book: FORGIVENESS Warner Books 1990. Used with permission.)

TYPES OF ABUSE

As we work with certain individuals, we often need to understand that part of their lives that put them in difficult situations. Abuse may be part of their picture. The following abuse information has been provided by **Friel & Counseling Associates**.

VICARIOUS ABUSE: A special case of abuse in which the victim is part of a family or other system where **SOMEONE ELSE** is abused in some way. This type of abuse can be just as damaging as actually being the recipient of the other types of abuse listed below.

EMOTIONAL ABUSE: Double binds (all choices are negative ones); Projection and transfer of blame; Alterations of the child's reality (intellectual abuse) "Dad's not drunk, he's just tired." Overprotection, smothering, excusing, blaming others for the child's problem; Fostering low self-esteem; Double messages "Of course, I love you, dear" while the body language says something else; Not talking about the abuse at all, as if it were not there.

EMOTIONAL NEGLECT: Failure to nurture, care for, or love the child; Failure to provide structure or set limits; Not listening to, hearing, or believing the child; Expecting the child to provide emotional nurturing to the parents, to make the parent feel good. "God sent you to take care of me." Not being emotionally present due to mental illness, chemical dependency, depression, or compulsivity.

PHYSICAL NEGLECT: Lack of food, clothes, shelter; Leaving a child alone in age-inappropriate ways or who is too young in charge of others; Failure to provide medical care; Allowing or encouraging the use of drugs, alcohol; Failure to protect the child from the abuse of others, including spouse.

VERBAL ABUSE: Excessive guilting, blaming, shaming, name-calling, put-downs, comparisons, teasing, making fun of, laughing at, belittling, nagging, screaming, verbal assault.

PHYSICAL ABUSE: Slapping, shaking, scratching, squeezing, hitting, beating with boards, sticks, belts, kitchen utensils, yardsticks, electric cords, shovel, hoses, etc.; throwing, pushing, shoving, slamming against walls or objects, burning, scalding, freezing, forcing of food or water, starving, having to watch others be physically abused, overworking.

SEXUAL ABUSE: Fondling, touching, innuendos, jokes, comments, looking, exposing self to, masturbating in front of, mutual masturbation, oral sex, anal sex, intercourse, penetration with fingers or objects, stripping and sexual punishments, pornography - taking pictures, or forcing the child to watch, forcing children to have sex with one another, enforced sexual activity with animals, watching others have sex, or be abused, sexual "games", sexual "torture," burning, etc.

ACTIVITY #20: <u>Small group discussion of types of abuse</u>. Working in triads or small groups of five or six, discuss situations where some form of abuse occurred and share what was done in the situation. What do you know now that could have been done! List some of the positive strategies used.

Option: As a large group presentation, ask for volunteers to role play the angry situation, as well as the behaviors that followed. Discuss the situation and strategies used to improve the situation. What was done to prevent you from becoming part of the problem by "feeding fuel into the fire?"

Young people, parents, and other adults need to learn how to detach from someone else's anger, and not internalize it and own it as being their fault. Problem ownership is very important in this case. Individuals sitting in their Indignation, Righteous Anger Stage of Forgiveness may be dumping all this anger on everyone around them, leaving others dancing away trying to figure out what to do next. One thing for certain is that <u>we must not become participants in this anger.</u> It is really the person's choice to be angry, not yours, so do not own it. Give them space to work it through.

Sometimes as we are doing our own recovery, or forgiveness work, these situations will serve as triggers for our own anger that we are desperately trying to get past. Individuals, or students that are children of alcoholics and have lived with too much anger in their lives, find it very difficult to behave well and not react to a teacher, or co-worker, who is also a child of an alcoholic. For that person, unreasonable anger may be the only way that they know to control another's behavior in certain situations, since that was all that was ever modeled by their parents.

So life in the classroom, or office, becomes a merry-go-round until someone in the room decides that if change is to occur, it must begin from within ourselves. We cannot change another person's behavior. We must learn to change our reactions to that behavior, since so many of our cycles and patterns are so predictable. It's like playing the same tape over and over. As the consequences for certain behaviors become clear, we can become cycle breakers and can look at the next stage of forgiveness, that of survivor.

STAGE V - SURVIVOR STAGE

You made it and you are now moving forward, taking charge and realizing that you have choices. You no longer need to wallow in your story. Yet you don't deny it. It can still be very tender for you. You know you did the best you could and you begin to believe that the person who hurt you did the best he or she could, even if his or her best was pretty bad.

You begin to reclaim your power over yourself and other people and you no longer need to feel controlled by this wrong. A sense of internal freedom sets in that strengthens you and challenges you to continue to believe in your self-worth.

You even begin to find that you have some time for play and your sense of humor returns. Your world begins to be a much brighter place and you feel much happier as you become less burdened.

(Adapted from Suzanne and Sidney Simon's book: FORGIVENESS Warner Books 1990. Used with permission.)

STAGE VI - INTEGRATION

Understanding how this experience fits into your whole life will help you to become who you are. "Yes, it happened to me; but it's not me; I'm more than it." If I am able to say that I am more than what the experience did to me, then I can also say that the person who caused me pain is more than that, too. Your self-esteem is in a better place now since you no longer identify yourself as a victim. Instead, you are a survivor ready to fly.

FORGIVENESS IS NOT:	FORGIVENESS IS:
Forgetting	Letting go
Condoning	Moving on
Suffering	Processing the healing
	Support Groups
Punishing	Coming to a place of peace within
Hanging on	Something we do for ourselves

(Adapted from Suzanne and Sidney Simon's book: FORGIVENESS Warner Books1990. Used with permission.)

Always remember that all of our life experiences, good and bad, have led us to this present moment where we are more sensitive to the needs of others suffering through these same issues. It is in sharing these feelings with others that we give them permission to feel and express themselves so that they may grow and become free from all that locks them in time and space.

THE PERSON WHO CAUSED US PAIN HAS GIVEN US THE GIFT OF UNDERSTANDING THE PAIN OF OTHERS GOING THROUGH THE SAME EXPERIENCE.

Explained in a simple way, I could not have written this book, if I had not lived through much of it in one way or another. It is difficult, if not impossible, for many of us to look at a series of bad experiences with a positive light. Yet, for those who have done their homework and have released themselves from being the victim and moved on with their lives, the richness that recovery brings allows them to again feel like a whole person and not like damaged merchandise. They will always understand where they have been and be sensitive to those who are still working through their process of recovery.

ACTIVITY #21: Letter of Forgiveness. Write a letter of forgiveness to yourself from a person who has hurt you and who has never said "I'm sorry." To often these letters are never written by that person even though time passes and you may feel you have forgiven them.

Write as quickly as you can without thinking of spelling, or punctuation. **This is a letter to you from the person who has hurt you.** Include in this letter all the things that you need them to say to you and trust that they are really being said. When you are through you may choose to share your letter with a partner.

Dear _____,

I know that I have hurt you in the past. I really never meant to do that to you. I need to tell you that now. . .

Adapted from Suzanne and Sidney Simon's book: FORGIVENESS Warner Books 1990. Used with permission.)

- CHAPTER 15 -

CREATING YOUR OWN REALITY WITH HEALTHY DETACHMENT

As we begin to see what is actually healthy and unhealthy behavior around us, we can also begin to choose what we will and will not allow into our lives. It actually becomes very clear to us, as we practice the language and self-talk that strengthens our conviction, not to fall back into the old patterns that trapped us. Healthy detachment with love allows us to take care of ourselves first so that we can then choose to help others.

If those around us are always negative, saying, "You can't do this, or you can't do that," we may have to be firm on our commitment to believe in ourselves and to do what we need to do for us. Only we can take a personal inventory of the things we have to change in us. We alone can decide how quickly, or slowly, we wish to work on them.

For me, creating my own reality meant that I had to let go of the illusions of what would never be and learn to accept the reality of what was. It also meant that within this new reality I had choices. I could pack up and move away from what was uncomfortable or I could detach in a healthy way from the behaviors that bothered me. I chose the latter. Changing locations, jobs, homes, does not always improve our situation until we become healthy enough to make these decisions.

I changed my attitude and shifted it from seeing only the negative side to working with only the good. My boundaries were set and I let go of the control that was preventing me from growing. As I now work my day, I get done what I can do. I do the best I can in every situation. If I fall short, that's okay! I recognize the things I cannot control and do not spend my energy trying to control them as I previously did!

JUST FOR TODAY (I HAVE A CHOICE)

- **JUST FOR TODAY** I will live through this day only, not tackling my whole life problem at once. I can do something at this moment that would appall me, if I felt that I had to keep it up for a lifetime.

- **JUST FOR TODAY** I will be happy, realizing that happiness does not depend on what others do or say, or what happens around me. Happiness is a result of being at peace with myself.

- **JUST FOR TODAY** I will adjust myself to what is - and not force everything to adjust to my own desires. I will accept my family, my friends, my business, my circumstances as they come.

- **JUST FOR TODAY** I will take care of my physical health; I will exercise my mind, I will read something spiritual.

- **JUST FOR TODAY** I will do somebody a good turn and not get found out - if anyone knows of it, it will not count. I shall do at least one thing I don't want to do, and I will perform some small act of love for my neighbor.

- **JUST FOR TODAY** I will go out of my way to be kind to someone I meet; I will be agreeable; I will look as well as I can, dress becomingly, talk low, act courteously, criticize not one bit, not find fault with anything, and not try to improve or regulate anybody except myself.

- **JUST FOR TODAY** I will have a program. I may not follow it exactly, but I will have it. I will save myself from two pests: hurry and indecision.

- **JUST FOR TODAY** I will stop saying, "If I had time." I never will "find time" for anything. If I want time I must take it.

- **JUST FOR TODAY** I will have a quiet time of

meditation wherein I shall think of God as I understand God, of myself, and of my neighbor. I shall relax and seek truth.

- **JUST FOR TODAY** I shall be unafraid. Particularly, I shall be unafraid to be happy, to enjoy what is good, what is beautiful, and what is lovely in life.

- **JUST FOR TODAY** I will accept myself and live to the best of my ability. I will choose to believe that I can live this one day.

- **THE CHOICE IS MINE.**

Author unknown

IN CONCLUSION:

DOES ANYONE HEAR OUR CRIES FOR HELP? We have touched on many issues from self-esteem and co-dependency to the dysfunctional system and their effect on our behavior and the behavior of those around us.

We have discussed the behaviors caused by chemical dependency and some of the action strategies that will help all of us to see our way out of owning, or trying to control, these behaviors: Letting go of the things in our lives we can not control, learning to set boundaries and follow through with consequences for these violation and healthy detachment.

All of these will help us to create our own reality as we forgive others for hurting us and forgive ourselves for not knowing any better! We must always remember:

1. **No one has the right to live "RENT FREE" in our heads** - taking over and controlling our every thought!

2. **No one has the right to violate our personal territory or boundaries.**

3. **"NO!"** is a word with a powerful meaning. It does not mean **"MAYBE,"** if you keep on asking. It does not mean **"YES"** if you are nice to me! **"NO!" MEANS "NO!"** - without an explanation!

4. **We need not compromise our self-esteem and personal power** by giving this power over to someone else. **Standing firm on our beliefs** can give us a strong sense of victory, as we fight the voices in our heads that may be pushing against us.

5. **We need to trust our instincts and our own value system** and follow its lead taking charge of our lives, as we once had, before we let others control us and destroy our feelings of self-worth.

As we start to gain support from people in our lives who share our vision, we will learn to detach in a healthy way from the negativity around us. We can then concentrate our energies on the more important things in life such as:

- Modelling the behavior you want from others
- Holding positive beliefs about human nature
- Setting high, but attainable, expectations
- Creating challenging and achievable goals
- Establishing a win-win atmosphere
- Acknowledging success and building a pattern for success
- Focus on excellence, not on perfection
- Keeping agreements you make without breaking promises
- Helping only when asked, tempered with judgment
- Allowing others to be responsible for their own learning and mistakes
- Encouraging others to become masters by becoming one yourself
- Developing an environment that includes sincere, positive affirmations
- Energize, energize, energize with positive thoughts and language!

As we move towards a more positive attitude towards ourselves and others, we will learn to not be as judgmental of ourselves and others and we will stay clear of the confrontations that engage us drag us backwards.

ACTIVITY #22: <u>Personal improvement list</u> of the things that you see in yourself that you need to change by completing the following statement:

If I wished to heighten my awareness of my need to change, I would

SELECTED READING LIST

Al-Anon Family Group Headquarters, Inc. **Twelve Steps of AA.** P.O. Box 182, Madison Square Station, New York, N.Y. 10159.

Beattie, Melody. **Codependent No More: How to Stop Controlling Others and Start Caring for Yourself.** Harper & Row, Publishers, Inc. 1987.

Black, Claudia. **It Will Never Happen To Me!** M.A.C. Printing and Publications Division, 1850 High Street, Denver, Colorado. 1981.

Bradshaw, John. **Bradshaw on: The Family: A Revolutionary Way to Self-Discovery.** Health Communications, Inc. Enterprise Center, 3201 SW 15th Street, Deerfield Beach, Florida. 33442. 1986.

Buscaglia, Leo F. **Loving Each Other: The Challenge of Human Relationships.** Ballantine Books, Division of Random House, Inc., N.Y. 1984.

Dean, Orvil. **The Co-dependent Educator.** Health Communications, Inc. En-terprise Center, 3201 SW 15th Street, Deerfield Beach, Florida. 33442. 1988.

Drews, Toby Rice. **Getting Them Sober: Vol. 1 & Vol. 2: A guide for Those Who Live With an Alcoholic.** Bridge Publishing, Inc. South Plainfield, New Jersey 07080. 1980.

Dyer, Wayne. **Gifts from Eykis: A Story of Self-Discovery.** Pocket Books, New York. 1983.

Forward, Susan and Joan Torres. **Men Who Hate Women & The Women Who Love Them: When Loving Hurts and You Don't Know Why.** Bantam Books, Inc. New York. 1987.

Gordon, Thomas. **P.E.T (Parent Effectiveness Training): Tested New Way To Raise Responsible Children.** New American Library, N.Y. 1975.

Kramer, Patricia. **Dynamics of Relationships: Guide For Developing Self-Esteem and Coping Skills. Two part series: Teacher/Student Manuals:** For Teens and Young Adults. Teacher/Student Manuals: Pre-teens and Young Children. 14526 Banquo Terrace, Silver Spring, MD 20906 1-800-438-0081.

Lowery, Don. **True Colors™ Books and Materials.** 2875 Sampson Avenue, Corona, California 91719. 1-800-422-4686.

Mitchell, Dr. William. **Power of Positive Students.** Bantam Books, Inc. (Paperback) 1986. Wm. Morrow & Co., N.Y. (Hardcover).

Myrick, Robert D. and Tom Erney. **Caring and Sharing: Becoming a Peer Facilitator.** Educational Media, Box 21311, Minn., MN. 1984.

Nelsen, Jane. **Positive Discipline: A Warm, Practical, Step-By-Step Source Book for Parents and Teachers.** Ballantine Books, Division of Random House, Inc., New York. 1987.

Norwood, Robin. **Women Who Loved Too Much: When You Keep Wishing and Hoping He'll Change.** Pocket Books, New York. 1985.

Paul, Jordan & Margaret Paul. **From Conflict To Caring: A Workbook for Do I Have To Give Up Me To Be Loved By You? & If You really Loved Me.** Comp-Care Publishers, 2415 Annapolis Lane, Minneapolis, Minnesota. 1988.

Powell, S.J., John. **Unconditional Love.** Argus Communications. One DLM Park Allen, Texas. 1978.

Rosellini, Gayle and Mark Worden. **Of Course You're Angry: Family Guide to Dealing With the Emotions of Chemical Dependence.** Hazelden Foundation. Harper & Row, San Francisco. 1985.

Simon, Suzanne and Sidney B. Simon. **Forgiveness-How to make peace with your past and get on with your life.** Warner Books, Inc 1990. Values Associates, 45 Mountain Road, Hadley, MA 01035.

Simon, Sidney B. **Vulture: A Modern Allegory on the Art of Putting Oneself Down.** Argus Communications, One DLM Park Allen, Texas. 1977.

Smith, Ann W. **Grand Children of Alcoholics:** Another Generation of Co-dependency. Health Communications, Inc. Enterprise Center, 3201 SW 15th Street, Deerfield Beach, Florida. 33442. 1988.

Sturkie, Joan. **Listening with Love: True Stories from Peer Counseling.** Resource Publications, Inc. San Jose, Ca. 1987.

Synowiec, Bertie, **Quick and Easy Self-Esteem Builders.** and **Group Facilitation Handbook** Positive Support Seminars, 28641 Elbamar, Grosse Ile, Michigan 48138. 1989. 1-800-676-3806.

Wegscheider-Cruse, Sharon. **Learning to Love Yourself: Finding Your Self-Worth.** Health Communications, Inc. Enterprise Center, 3201 SW 15th Street, Deerfield Beach, Florida. 33442.

Whitfield, Charles. **Healing the Child Within: Discovery and Recovery for Adult Children of Dysfunctional Families.** Health Communications, Inc. Enterprise Center, 3201 SW 15th Street, Deerfield Beach, Florida. 33442.

Woititz, Janet Geringer. **Adult Children of Alcoholics.** Health Communications, Inc. 2119-A Hollywood, Florida. 1983.

Vitale, Barbara Meister. **Unicorns Are Real: A Right-Brained Approach to Learning.** Jalmar Press, 45 Hitching Post Drive, # 2, Rolling Hills Estates, Ca. 90274.

LIST OF ACTIVITIES